RAGING GRACE

Australian writers speak out on disability

First published in 2024
Published by Puncher and Wattmann
PO Box 279
Waratah NSW 2298
www.puncherandwattmann.com
web@puncherandwattmann.com

ISBN 9781923099326

Cover art: Rachael Wenona Guy
Cover design: Miranda Douglas
Text design and typesetting: Miranda Douglas
Proofreading: Esther Ottaway
Printed by Ingram Spark

A catalogue record for this book
is available from the National Library of Australia.

This project has been assisted by the Australian Government through
Creative Australia, its principal arts investment and advisory body.

RAGING GRACE

Australian writers speak out on disability

edited by

Andy Jackson, Esther Ottaway, Kerri Shying

Puncher & Wattmann

Acknowledgements

The writing within this project emerged out of the Writing the Future of Health Fellowship, under the auspices of RMIT University's Health Transformation Lab. As Fellow, Andy Jackson facilitated workshops and discussions with the writers in the anthology. He's profoundly grateful to all the staff at the Lab for their trust and support.

"Pandemic Year 3" by CB Mako and Beau Windon; "Perennially gaslit, the disabled reject humanity" by Esther Ottaway; "Instructions for the broken" by Andy Jackson; "Dis-topia" by Andy Jackson and Alex Creece; and "Branches" by Kit Kavanagh-Ryan, Sarah Stivens, Leah Robertson, Beau Windon, Jess Kapuscinski-Evans and Angela Costi (arranged by Andy Jackson), were first published in *Meanjin* (Summer 2022) in an essay by Andy Jackson, "Diagnosing Tomorrow: Collaborative Writing from the Future of Health".

"Rare" by Angela Costi and Andy Jackson was first published in *Griffith Review 80: Creation Stories* (2023).

"Uncertain Parts" by Angela Costi and Leah Robertson, "My raucous, singing ear" by Rachael Wenona Guy and Heather Taylor-Johnson, "Joy to my world" by Kerri Shying and Esther Ottaway, and "ECT Tree" by Anna Jacobson and Gemma Mahadeo were first published in *Cordite 106: Open* (2022).

"Crack and Burn" by Sarah Stivens and Jasper Peach, and "Debris" by Leah Robertson and Andy Jackson were first published in *Australian Poetry Journal Vol.12 No.1 Divergence, Relevance* (2022).

"Questing Beast" by Michèle Saint-Yves and Robin M Eames; "Walking Document" by Ruby Hillsmith and Beau Windon; "Coalescent" by Beau Windon, Andy Jackson, Michèle Saint-Yves, Robin M Eames and Ruby Hillsmith, were all first published in *Rabbit 37: Collaborations* (2023).

"how do we protect the mutant from annihilation by the 'normal'?" by Gaele Sobott and Andy Jackson was first published in *Massachusetts Review Vol.63 No.4: Disability Justice* (2022).

"After writing a book on female autism, I decide to bury it" by Esther Ottaway and "After reading her poem, I remember the diagnosis they give me" by Andy Jackson were first published in *Island 166* (2022). They were also selected for *Best of Australian Poetry* 2023, edited by Gig Ryan and Panda Wong.

"Objects of Illness/Recovery" by Anna Jacobson and Katerina Bryant was first published in *Island* (online, 2023).

"Betrayal" by Bron Bateman and Andy Jackson was first published in *The Saturday Paper* (August 26, 2023).

"Our Pain, Our Whimsy" by Sarah Stivens and Alex Creece was first published in *Canberra Disability Review* (Edition 8: Summer 2023).

All these poems were written on the various sovereign lands of indigenous nations. We pay respect to Elders, past and present, and acknowledge their ongoing custodianship of Country and their resistance to colonisation.

Contents

Foreword in three parts

1.

Confession: I've always been somewhat of a soloist. There are reasons for that, concentric circles. Introversion. A bruised psyche, having felt the punch of too many stares and remarks. Capitalist, neoliberal insistence on self-reliance. Habit.

But – and I should have known – the stories that we tell ourselves, and the stories we're told, aren't carved in stone. Or if they are, the persistent drip and flow of water can do its liberatory, erosive work.

In late 2021, RMIT University's Health Transformation Lab opened submissions for their inaugural Writing the Future of Health Fellowship. The Black Summer bushfires were still sickeningly fresh in the memory. The COVID pandemic was overwhelming, in every sense of the word. It was obvious that the air we share was not a metaphor, but a precipitous reality. We survive only if we are cared for, by governmental and social systems, by our neighbours, by strangers, by those willing to commit to a collective health.

In my application for the fellowship, titled "The Future of Health is Collab/Oration", I wrote this:

> In this context, technological and pharmacological interventions will continue to be important, yet these interventions can only truly promote health where the medical system – and the broader society – listens to those whom it purports to serve. Disability may be experienced in individual bodies, but it is created and amplified (and potentially alleviated) by social forces and relationships. It is cemented in the silencing or marginalisation of disabled voices. The future of health, then, depends on disabled people being allowed a genuine voice.

I was fortunate to be announced, early in 2022, as the Fellow. My proposal was to write collaborative poems and essays with a range of other writers who are disabled, are neurodivergent and/or experience chronic illness. Workshops and conversations would lead to affinities and contrasts being explored in pairs or more of thinking, feeling people. We would diagnose the present and imagine therapeutic futures. Health in the broadest sense, on our terms.

The success of the project would depend not so much on its design, though that would be important, but on its participants. We needed to be a genuinely diverse group, in terms of experience, place of residence, cultural background, gender, sexuality, and age. In Australia's disability communities at the moment, there's a wealth of talent and breadth of insight, so it was pretty easy to build a long list of writers to invite. Some couldn't make it, were too busy (a too-common predicament for many writers, especially those who know ill-health), or were unsure whether the project's focus on disability fitted them. I admire their self-awareness and care. But most leapt at the invitation.

I'm immensely grateful that the Health Transformation Lab saw merit in the idea of collaboration. This project has been transformative for me as a writer, a workshop facilitator, and as a human. I wrote things I would never have written alone, perhaps because I learnt a little more about how to listen (and how easy it is to assume).

Above all, though, I'm hugely proud of this anthology and the writers within it. Within each collaboration, there's an amplification, a multiplication, where each writer draws out of the other something unexpected and transcendent. Yes!, yes!, they say. Or, yes!, yes!, and also...! Not only the cacophonous uncertainties of public space, but the ambivalent fullness of our homes. Not only medical gaslighting, but the joy of wheelchairs. Not only gardening, but the soil of the digital. Myths, insects, synapses, keloids, bird nests, masks, and transformations. Ampersands and ellipses everywhere.

I hope this book prompts more books like it. The project – considered in the broadest sense as a working towards the most capacious solidarity, towards disability justice committed to the entire web of life – is ongoing. The writing-together has fuelled a desire for more writing-together, but it has also brought each of us back to our own individual voice, refreshed. *Raging Grace,* then, includes some individual works, interspersed with the collaborative, that reflect on possible futures and subterranean nows.

Thanks finally to my co-editors Kerri Shying and Esther Ottaway, whose honesty, trust, insight and humour during the assembling of this book kept my feet on the earth, and my eyes facing forward.

Andy Jackson

2.

I can think of no one better to imagine the future of health than writers and poets, who not only illuminate complex medical and social issues, but who can wield excellent writing's superpower – that of entering and deeply moving us, so that we empathise, so that we care. As a woman, for whom medical treatment is often lacking or ineffective, because most research is done on men; as an autistic person, for whom cognitive and physical dysregulation defines my daily existence; and as a parent of, and advocate for, an autistic daughter, I have much to say on health, disability, and the behemoth systems which dominate them. When Andy asked me to join his Writing the Future of Health collaborative group, I jumped at the chance.

The Zoom meetings we held to create these works were extraordinary. We were battling to be present: during the meetings people had blood sugar attacks, migraines, vertigo, panic attacks, suffered through pain, left the screen to warm up heat packs and take medications, and attended while lying down. People turned their screens off and their sound down when in sensory overwhelm, but were present in chat; people logged on late because they were ill, and logged off early because they'd become ill, then used email or texts to share thoughts.

And it felt, gloriously, like home. These people totally understood, when I arrived in my dressing-gown, that I was still seriously working on the project. They knew, when I wasn't present in the meeting, that I was still working hard on the project. Rather than running to a schedule, we worked in a symbiotic flow, using the quorum that was present in each moment, people finding manifold ways to be heard and seen in a web of connection and acceptance and multiform communication that was almost its own organism. I'd never worked in an environment like it.

The disabled are always working, and always looking for those rare sweet spots of energy and functionality to arrive so that they can download that work into the world. Fertile collaborative writing emerged between writers, which led on to reading sessions over Zoom. Here we heard these nascent pieces, works born of difficulty, works which were both vulnerable and fierce, spoken out loud for the first time. Having walked our own years-long paths of disability, paths which, as Andy has said, are excoriatingly solitary, we found deep validation in one another's pain, and energy in one another's aliveness and outspokenness. We were brought often to tears; and I will never forget the electric moment when Jasper Peach read aloud their phrase which so brilliantly encapsulates the disability experience, *raging grace*. The chat went wild, as we instantly recognised it to be the luminous title of this volume.

When I reflect on the works in this collection, what stands out to me, even more than their intelligence, cogency and craft, is how creative they are. How extraordinarily creative. The works, some in fiction, non-fiction, and free verse forms, some in hybrid forms, and some in forms never-before seen, shine with innovative and clever ways of telling. When I thought about this, I realised that I shouldn't be surprised at it: disabled people and those with chronic ill health are used to being creative. We are used to having to invent creative solutions to a multitude of problems every day. We are used to being innovators, rigging workarounds, hacking the so-called "normal" ways of doing things and of moving through the world. We fit no system, and are not afraid of making a path where there is none. So our writing, too, is creative and multifarious.

Disability consciousness is still very, very new. I'm a member of Generation X, which is described as "self-sufficient, results-oriented and hard-working": a generation which was taught to see disability as failure, illness as weakness. Nor is Australian culture one where you talk about disability. What emerges from the writing in this volume is an indictment of a medical system, and of individuals within it, which communicate to the disabled and chronically ill that we are failures. That we are weak people, just not strong-minded enough or self-disciplined enough to be healthy. I invite readers to see, through this extraordinary written work, how iron-willed, resilient, courageous, dignified, and joyful we are. Yes, we are raging – we have to be; yet we are also the epitome of grace.

Esther Ottaway

3.

The something different about me isn't really my ethnicity, sexuality or disability, it's far more basic. I wasn't raised to be an individual. I think culture has a lot to do with how you come to collaborative work, which for me is a vital part of community and family. Nothing is achieved alone, as anyone who grew up in a large family (and a small house) will tell you; at the very least, we must co-operate to communicate. Disability is a beautiful Frankenstein, as Andy says – muscular and of diverse parts. It's a mistake to assume consensus in a group of people with disability; we're from all kinds of backgrounds and mindsets, with different politics and allegiances.

Peers and peer work have been a way inside hidden or hiding populations for a long time; the term describes the non-hierarchical process of knowledge sharing and community building by people who recognise each other as belonging to a shared identity.

That feeling courses through you like electricity, pouring even from the small iPad screen. The first meeting, on a Sunday, we're staggering in, in our own time, laying down, propped on cushions, recognising the other worlds like ours, it's home. Writing, well that's another matter. Scary. We've all learnt to write as loners. We are luckily the long distance runners of fear, and we dive in, writing in pairs, in thrupples, in sinuous spirals, columns of call and response, a church of anger, joy, grief, exploration and lust.

While editing this book two things emerged clearly. The first was that possession of a medical condition was not in itself a disability, a fact I knew from my own experience of living with a chronic disabling condition. Disability is a combination of a person with a condition and the world they live in. The second was that our pairs and thrupples of writers didn't necessarily see their disability as the main pain in a situation – or indeed their main identity. Like wearing a pair of too-tight pants then blaming the leg for the chafe, it's arse-around to think that disability is always the root of the problem – something to be 'fixed'. In the words of Trisha Hersey, "I do nothing alone, my whole life is a collaboration". One of the brands of P94 mask I rely on for my safety has this printed on it; "we are the waves of the same sea the people of the same earth".

As a group we experienced greater stress with regard to income, housing stability, unmet or unstable care needs and discrimination. The wide net cast by Andy across the country among writers with disability seemed to back up these statistics from the ABS. We are parents, men, women, trans, non-binary, teachers, lawyers, queers, artists and we recoiled at our main identity being decided for us by a medical assumption. Working together in peer groups, in crip time, melted and transformed how we spoke to and about ourselves.

There are those who find themselves wishing for greater entrance into the 'standard' world, and those to whom this world is hostile, rude and inexplicable. Universal experiences of misogyny in medicine, good lookers getting more attention; there's no chin-up positivity here. Some of us want to hide, some of us, since Covid-19, have to. Freedom from discrimination is hard to find in mainstream life and more so since the pandemic. This hyper-capitalist Western world is often threatening of people with difference, and who seem not to fit the mould of 'individual work unit, ready for action'. We are likely to be judged as deserving or undeserving of charity according to our attitudes and responses to the world around us. The phrase 'pre-existing conditions' as a rationale for death on the daily became a recurrent blow for many people who continue to be at heightened risk. Safe places seem hard to find.

The reassertion of individualism couldn't come fast enough for many in the mainstream. Individual effort and the ability of the body to reflect your own efforts rather than chance is central to Western dream-spaces. The emphasis on individual achievement leaves unexplored this inherent need and talent for collaboration. We come to collaboration, I think, despite our backgrounds, by merit of disability – it does after all, take a lot of collaboration and co-operation to diagnose and strategise for equality in our lives. An ease with teamwork, (our team-need) is not valued in the system which surrounds us. In the 'quest and restitution' narrative of life, chaotic and collaborative collective effort seems strange and subversive.

In a sense the Covid pandemic and the subsequent 'new normal' underlined the collaborative nature of human health; with science, with the community, with the elements of nature. The discomforting understanding that emerged was our interdependence on each other. Interdependence equates to vulnerability. And vulnerable we are, in a world unused to the combination of power and vulnerability. These poems and prose pieces chart the joy, pain, horror, idiocy, fury, and soft comforts of our normal lives. The works are unique, insistent and embedded in the physical knowledge of collaboration as lived experiences.

There is joy. Collaboration is after all a group of individuals working together for a common goal. We hope that when you've finished *Raging Grace* you enjoy the conversations as much as we have.

Kerri Shying

Dis-topia

At first, I disfigured it'd be a brief trend, shallow
fetish or disability signalling. But requests kept coming.
My inbox was crippled, in the way we mean it now,
as in abundant, brilliant. Someone wanted to break
into modelling, so which surgeon would I recommend
for crafting them a hump? Did I know any neurodiverse
sensory architects who weren't fully booked out? Another
wanted my help with the syllabus for an able-bodied
conversion program. I should have them fill out an online
deform, with a captcha that tests their normality. Let's
deface it, like many of us, I was tired, confused, beautiful.

The neurotypes sign up for therapy, eager
to adhere to my social abnorms. Let's get freakified.
They once banished me to aspurgatory, now they beg
me to treat their dysfunctional impairments. They stare
at me in envy, no longer disgust or bewilderment.
I teach them to read the lines, skip the in-betweens. I thread music
through their smooth, songless bodies. Embrace their
maladaptive daydreams and behavioural blips.
Unmask their neurotic erotics, somatic dramatics.
They undertake my process of maddening, which is
to say intensifying, glittering, honeying.

Andy Jackson & Alex Creece

Awry

Sometimes nothing feels awry. Not for a whole
day, but a cluster of moments, as the light
seems, impossibly, to hold

Sometimes everything feels awry;
the days, made-up clusters of moments
are not all darkness. They are as absolute
as antimatter.

My wardrobe spans size near-anorexic to
watch-your-cholesterol-level obese. Its ability to
annoy immediate family is my inability or
apparent refusal to update to latest fashions.

(I mean it, this isn't poetic
license, some angle of delicate light
can hold –
though I can't hold it)

Two, three a.m. The dark is a consoling stillness.
A loving cat, nagging for their human
to slide under bedclothes.
A finger, or three, of whisky,
with a too-big bowl of ice cream.
Gratitude for a pet's unconditional love, and
momentary hedonism is my occasional prayer.

and expand. A shirt that fits. A gaze,
landing softly for once. Another mouthful of dark
ale, and a fridge surprise meal that
ended up much better than we expected.
The fact that I can say 'we'

still stops me in my potholed tracks.

The times there is no cat to wake up to,
professionals bring water and medications
to your bedside. A private psych ward is *not* a hotel.

Fasting overnight; starving, barely awake at dawn
yet needing to be conscious to be rendered unconscious,
when your turn comes last. Counting to four;
a darkness very much needed.

There's been too much time lost to hospitals,
on our backs, waiting for the whiteness

of the ceiling to come down and fix us.
As if. The whole thing is impaired, and I know
my ache is not your pain, which is
not their suffering. Why do I think myself alone?

I am too hard/difficult/complicated to be
a (daughter, a sibling, a(n aunt), a wo/m(a)n.

Circling us, the new moon, bittersweet pill

So often, am alone, and always
lonely. Will ECT continue long enough
to disrupt menses?

that wants to swallow us.
I have learnt to internalise.
(Man.) (Less than.)
I am trying to quieten
this murmur in my bones,
so I can listen.

Every single muscle aches in chorus
from the microcramps of convulsion.
No menstruation, no PMDD symptoms;
its cessation brings about
temporary gender euphoria:
I am not supposed to celebrate this.

Andy Jackson & Gemma Mahadeo

My Raucous, Singing Ear

On the Train

I'm sitting on a blue seat, two red ones in front of me and a sign above them illustrating what priority seating looks like. Outside the window of the metro train, the day speeds past the planted trees, the parked cars, cottages, cafes, bicycles and prams. Red is for a person with half a leg and a crutch, and it looks as though the crutch has morphed into the person's arm. Disability is all sorts of body parts, I see no need to linger. I am heading to the city, wearing boots that rise to my knees, protecting my ankles from excess atoms bouncing off one another with such fury they're bound to trip me up. Red is for the person with a ball-tipped cane in one hand and lead attached to a dog in the other. The outline of the animal makes me think of my dog, and for a second I forget how fast we're going. There will be a lot of people in the city, each one trying to match the other's pace. As a group, it will look like they're chasing after the rolling cars but haven't the stamina or grace. I'm dealing with the sensorially complex; it doesn't have to be rational. A red seat is for the person bent at the knees, spine at an angle, leaning on a stick shaped like a giant candy cane. And there will be noise in the city, invasive as rockets. Red for those with large bellies harbouring babies that haven't a clue what they're getting into, how each scream at the time of their birth will blast new light into their world. There will be traffic noise and footsteps and birdcalls and alarms and voices talking; the wind will mingle with every leaf; insects buzzing on the breeze. The sign says to please remember that not all disabilities are visible. The vibrations of the train are in my head, like the city will be with all those rushing feet, my knee-high boots in slow-mo, trying to catch the rotation. There is no image of what a person with invisible disability might look like.

my flannel dress
my mounded breasts
my ever-growing beauty mole
the holes in my ears

my grandfather's eyes
my head-top bun
my thinking brain
my dimpled thighs
these inner frights
my just-cut nails

these eating teeth
this gobbled mess
these pounds of flesh
this healthy tan

In the Car

Today I can drive. Yesterday I could not. The steering wheel in my hands is warm as victory. Driving can trigger vestibular migraine. Driving is sensorially taxing, a rush of movement, sound and light that sends my mind spangling into vertiginous places. As I drive my field of vision lights up with crimson and blue spots, raining fragments of silver, moving like crazed fish. My muscles begin to clench. My hands become weak and uncoordinated. I lurch. I cease to be able to focus, see straight. I can't take in what I'm looking at. The rushing ribbon of road makes my eyes throb and my brain cramp. Now I can't comprehend our conversation. I can't hear you. Consumed by the high-pitched ringing of my ears, nerves, skin. There's a riot in my brain. Eyes drift out of focus, my jaw locks. I fall into a blizzard of my own senses, competence erased. I pull over to rest. Driving is a nauseating act of will, movement, a kind of screaming. The body's trajectory through space, a sensorial assault. But you wouldn't know it. On the surface I look ordinary. On the surface I am just another person at the wheel moving from A to B.

my sombre clothes
blockish frame
my middle age
this greying mane

these rapid breaths
and busy hands
these blinking eyes
determined jaw

these trembling limbs
my singing brain

familial hymns:
allodynia *hyperalgesia*
migraine

At the Butcher

I have three children, fair, pale and risen lean, and I'm always buying chicken, what it means to be a mother in this suburb. The butcher's a warehouse of undignified echoes, refrigeration everywhere, and oh my tender ear – even when I flinch nothing shuts-up, and there go my squinting eyes, as if changing the shape of my vision will help, and I need help, at the butcher, with the tilting. But I've got this, only slabs of breast, slimy limbs, cleaved wings, these butchered bodies I've never intended to understand: *I am owning this chore*. Though it's funny / not funny how I got from there to here in a minute's time. And yet here's another level of there-to-here, and just like that, another. I own nothing, a silent beggar, the coins in my purse so valueless I've forgotten they even exist. By now everyone should be staring because I'm freakish, primal like an animal deprived of its howl, and staring is what's done when people are afraid of someone like me, lets them bask in the knowledge that they're intact, but they're not staring, no one is, and it's Tuesday at the butcher, there's anxiety at the butcher, and I have become the centre of my thinking which means telling the butcher what I want is a beastly task, the worst thing I've had to do all day, and I wonder: can she tell there's something wrong with me? Can the butcher see my disability?

the eczema below my nose
these spandex clothes
my thirsting throat

this slowing breath
these red cheeks
the purple runners   on my feet

my unshaved legs
my ankle tattoo
my niggling fear
my raucous ear
my wiggling belly
this middle age
this healthy breath
on the whiff
of raw meat   sensitivity

At the Supermarket

I have avoided supermarkets for three months now. The physio says it is very normal for people in my situation to become *shop-shy* – too much visual information to process, too many bright lights, the disorientating architecture of aisles. *But you must*, she says, *persist and treat your daily tasks as rehab*. So today I am attempting a grocery shop. Hovering outside the entry, my heart flips, sweat pools on my forehead. *No*, I tell myself firmly, *we are doing this*! I pick up a red plastic basket, sweep into the glittering tumble of sensory chaos. Logos and fonts vie for attention, some loud, plump, and brazen, some earthy and restrained. I prefer wrappers that are less colourful and papery to touch, retaining some hush when handled. I avoid glitz and plastic like a bombast at a party. My basket has some items in it – I'm doing well. How many aisles can I stare down without the spin beginning in my brain, my right ear ringing or my legs crumpling? Row upon row of aisles stretch before me. I am bathed in sound, the chatter/clatter of shoppers, shrill scanners at checkout, muzak. I pass the deli, try not to retch at the pink hue of shaved ham, the salty, cheesy, meaty odours co-mingling that always remind me of public toilets, ghosts of menstruation, sweating groins – something heavy and faecal. Approaching the dairy section, I'm in trouble; swivelling my head from side-to-side to eye rows of milk, vertigo begins. Suddenly I'm slightly out of body, my footing uncertain. My vision lurches and swamps, my limbs become weak. I stand still and look at the floor, a hot flush overtakes me. I keep my eyes lowered and try to centre myself by feeling my feet on the ground. I remain there for a while until I don't feel like I'm falling off the highwire of my own existence. The basket in my sagging arm tilts.

my sweating face
this triggering place
my spinning head
public dread
these reddened cheeks
unsteady legs,   these rocking feet
faltering hands

my flicking eyes
this raucous ear
my quickening breaths
this basket, laden

At Home

I am couch-sprawled, pinch of lower back and hips because I twist my body outlandishly, a comfort that's uncomfortable. Every night I cuddle into this, the sofa black, plush and velvety, except where the cushioned edges have an oil-slick sheen. The armrests are the same, sleek and loved, and they're wide and solid, sturdy enough to hold the heftiest, most fragile glass of wine, which it does, nightly, usually a red though sometimes a white because I have cravings, options, just enough money and a strong and defiant will. My acupuncturist / therapist / saviour / friend helps me rationalise my excess: *people all over the world try to cut down their drinking and most aren't dealing with an invisible disability; give yourself a break*, and I do. It's true, I give myself a lot of breaks. My hair is still wet from an hour-plus bath where I read a book of poetry, my partner and children just fine without me (just fine, just fine, without me, great). I am a series of brief indulgences. I gift myself minor freedoms from a tough trudge because my trudging is ongoing. I see myself deserving of this every single night which feels selfish and reactive and I think it's okay to be both of these things. I think it's okay to take over the couch.

my leggings and ugg boots
my fire-warmed cheeks
my coming down
my tired frown
this digital tv my raucous ear

the remote control
my spiralling hole
my sloshing gut

and wallowing and swallowing

my bloodshot eyes
my throat-blocked tears
my melting endurance
this insisting endurance

this exhaustion
this assent
and I think I've seen
this show before

At Home

I open the front door, smell the familiar woody aroma of home, feel warmth enveloping me. Home is a place of contradictions, it's where I feel acutely alone and vulnerable, yet, most deeply known and loved. Home knows all of me; tired, sick, depressed, angry, joyful, hilarious – mortal. At home I am at my best and worst, and like a lover I know too well, proximity can breed contempt. Yet, here is my touchstone, my stability – the place I face my limits. These walls have held my despair and fatigue; the big blue couch, my prone body; this pillow, my tears. I've walked the small gamut of these rooms dreaming of larger more able-bodied territories. I've also nestled into the space of this house willingly, felt gratitude for its shelter, welcomed the limits of a contained world. Within these porous old walls have rained my sorrows, captivity but also my love – the hard-won moments of unremarkable ordinariness and transcendence; the cup and kettle, favourite blanket, resident birds, the voice of my beloved … our shared meals, our cat, her nightly solicitation for lap, her dawn calls for food and us.

my woollen slippers

moth-bitten shrug
my coming-down
this steaming cup

the evening meal I dice and cut

our mewling cat

these aching limbs my singing ear vision swims

home again

another day within this house

his soft warm voice and temperance

my inclement skin restlessness

I've seen all this
before

Heather Taylor-Johnson & Rachael Wenona Guy

Rare

Here are some other stories. I made my home at the outskirts of the temple complex, out of the way of the priests, but sitting where pilgrims could see me as they approached, a tin cup to catch coins, my body a warning and a promise. Or, I appeared unremarkable at my birth, until my bones began to grow in an impetuous fashion, torso clenching into a fist, pressing my heart and lungs into a space too small. Or, I survived, but in a remote cave, smudged with a mystical bitterness, visited by other outcasts, whose hands reached out to touch my hunched back for prophecy or consolation. Or maybe I was never born, the prenatal test results causing a look of concern on the doctor's face which my mother couldn't resist falling into. I have to tell you these things that never happened – or what happened to others like me, and will happen again – before I can think of what did. For too long, I have felt alone in this body. The past, an inaccessible crypt. The future, a mirage.

There are many ways to carry a story. My father smothered his stories with bravado. Here he is, laughing at the sea drenching him on the deck. There he is, shoving money at the doctor to cure his dying mother. Another time, his chest deflated when the nurse reached for the pink blanket. His survival was never one step at a time. It was the leap, the stumble, the fall. Another form of inheritance. When my home was a hospital for too many nights, he left the visits to mother. I felt her walk the corridor towards me. She said, you know your father. I knew him. His struggle to tell another story of scarred shame.

A genetic counsellor got me to search my kinship for answers. She said, among your greats and your grands, your firsts seconds and thirds, those long dead and those estranged, look for their lesions. I scoured doctor's letters about my Pappou's cancer. I spoke to Cousin Mary about her goiter. I visited a distant aunty in Cyprus who was said to grow nuggets under her skin. I returned with a book of doubts. I was told, your aunt's angiolipoma is not related to your colony. My body is viewed as an isolated island. Divided by warring factions. I will monitor their skirmishes, hoping for peace.

I have disappointed my partner, and myself, with this myopia about the future, my impaired ability to dream. A thick fog, stubborn and cold. It's almost all I've known. When I was first handed my diagnosis – a cumbersome package I could barely hold, let alone lift, which smelt of dirt and smoke – I was told people like me tended to die in their thirties or forties. About that, they were wrong. But I still carry this thing around, stopping now and then to tear another layer of wrapping off, unsure exactly what I will find underneath it all. Is this shape a heart or an icon? Brain or egg? And what is pecking, wriggling, frantic to escape?

The present, tales told unblinking. As mother refuses to fall off Alzheimer's cliff. She continues the story of how I swam out of her. A slippery fish, we couldn't catch you. I cradle this story more than the others about me. This is the story of how I truly attempted escape. Those eight months in her womb were not buoyed with hope. Intensive lessons were drilled from her to me. Courses on ancestry, history, tradition were packed into bite-sized burdens. A miracle I emerged with torso. They counted ten fingers and toes. Sighed their relief. Left me swaddled in the crib. Learning to feel the pinch and pull of cells squabbling. Then they gave me to geology. A child carries the grief of families – from war and famine – by growing a body of rocks.

My family preferred stories that came from the television to the ones of our own bodies. Here I am bent over, congested with them. The one where I'm afraid of the scalpel, anticipating the probing of gloved hands. My mother swallowing tears as she walked away, down the hospital corridor. The heavy, lulling bliss of anaesthetic, arms out for a taste of burial. How I imagined corrective surgery might solve everything, from ill-fitting shirts to the loneliness of being visible. So many stories, competing, another survival of the fittest. Fit, not as in strong, but as in appropriate, adaptive. I want every deformed story, scarred, ashamed, to find its niche. My father, buried so long now. All those interrupted ones. Let them hold me as I hold them.

I think of a colony of termites, their mouthparts at my cartilage, aorta, the lenses that allow me to see this world. Other times, what comes to mind is a fierce seed, poised to germinate and bloom into alien beauty. Metaphors fail us as much as bodies. Still we persist. Marfan may be a genetic baton, but it has always been my bones, my very material. I am here because it is determined to be part of the human story, and because I have not been overwhelmed. I am extracting the resources I need from it. Each time I come back up to the surface smudged, shaky. Wanting kin, a species of future.

This is baby. Doesn't stop crying. Will never escape my body. Suckles on ancestral fright. In my twenties, the doctor christened it Schwannoma. Not lump or stone or cyst or hairball. A name to misspell. A name to pummel into the pillow when sleep eludes. A name to throw at the blank wall. Schwannoma grew to recalcitrant teen. Never a Yes to my No. Fooling my leg to limp in my thirties. Reaching for GrandPappou's cane in my forties. In my fifties, I seek to know its gender, its story, its intention with my body. I ask these questions to my thinning skin.

Andy Jackson & Angela Costi

Steps like knives

muscles fray to
silt—water glassthick
and heavy,
blood new-spilt
from your body.
Split tendons re-
woven, wire shining as you
cut the surgeon's hand
on each new
cracking
arch.

I'll see what I can make
from you she says
hands
splayed on your scale,
your throat
working—tongue
numbed down
to nothing.
hopestruck
and waiting
for tomorrow's ache.

red spirals out from silver
all bound up
with thread.

I didn't want to be found
here   you and I   trade cures
they leave
on our tongues   after
they've ~~taken adjusted~~ fixed
what they need   revenge
is a cramp in Frankenstein's wrist
a needle slip
yes   we can want
all this but still to be made
again

Constellations of starch
and cannula   blanket us
we whisper
          to new fragments
recite them a home

You're first   I heard
the monitors go   dark
last scrape   of curtain rings
nurse jokes about forgetting
a graduation cap

You smiled
I said goodbye to your stitches.

Sarah Stivens & Kit Kavanagh-Ryan

Congenital
(trans planted)

This child could grow   a tail if it wanted to
(*The Origin of Species* stays splayed only eighty leaves in
snake-spined   who gave you permission   to be
smeared and fine.   Mid-century facsimile, the writing
funny like that   tortured by backpacks and photographers
worse than mine, skeleton-worn, down hollow and
would you stop   tilting   your head
the scientist observes
This body was always revolting   against itself
That wingtip   those ribs
lizard-skinned   why can't you just   use soap
glossed and wired   shining beneath   the taxidermist's art
like the rest of us   Vaseline hands slipping   off the keyboard
transfigured through graphite
would you stop   leaving   a mark
as I let the pages crumple and tear   through a dead child's lens).

Sarah Stivens & Kit Kavanagh-Ryan

Grace: Gardeners and Listeners

Caring doctors who listen with empathy are gold. While these rare doctors are the future, we need to weed out the other kind that are proliferating – doctors who give shocking treatment, verbal abuse, emotional and medical trauma, and gaslight their patients. It's time for patients to stop spending decades trying to find 'the right fit' of health care professionals when all we are searching for is someone who can do their job with compassion. The weeding-out process needs to start at the grassroots level. Students training to become specialists, doctors, psychiatrists, psychologists, or nurses, must undertake Narrative Medicine before entering into professional practice. Narrative Medicine – the creation of empathy between doctor and patient through storytelling, is an expanding field in America, and forms a new subject in medical degrees. Medicine students are encouraged to journal, to understand their patients and their situation in a more holistic way. This needs to be compulsory, so that those with appalling bedside manner and abysmal patient-listening skills will fail, and never enter into face-to-face consultation with clients, who deserve better. This needs to happen in Australia. More can still be done to diversify Narrative Medicine to create a better future for patients. Patients' own writing, artwork, and storytelling expressing lived experiences is the answer to creating understanding and empathy. Only then can Narrative Medicine operate at a higher level. Doctors must therefore gain visual literacy and written comprehension skills to understand the patient's story, not through verbal communication alone. Doctors who treat their patients like specimens, without respect, brandishing authority, who judge, and lack care, nuance, and sensitivity, have no place in the future of our health. That world is over. The future of health is empathy. No longer will we be trees strangled on our way to accessing help. But we need gardeners in our universities and institutions pulling out the weeds, stopping the spread of poisonous negligence, enabling patient-centred care to flourish, so we can grow on our own terms. We hold power and knowledge in our lived experience of our own body and mind. It's time for healthcare professionals to listen. Training has only just begun.

Anna Jacobson

You can find her

settling
on a diagnosis   straight   out of Instagram
softening the blow   with emojis
the psych makes it real

kneeling
at the altar   of another public toilet
escaping the   ~~noise people panic~~ heat
tiles   agreeing to be friends

wishing
for sunglassesto survive the supermarket
for brain fog to clear
for someone to make the bed
for the cat to talk
for rest

You can find her   learning
not to fight   the body   let it shiver
with delight   stim given permission

fumbling
through labels and medications
in schoolyards and doctors' offices
new names   for   old insults

fighting
through   muck and madness
drowning in   ~~lights trauma action~~ inertia
the world   as a nemesis

hiding
from well-intended cliches
from old stereotypes
from textbook pathology
from herself
from you

You can't find her
~~You can't find her~~
~~You can't find her~~

Sarah Stivens & Alex Creece

Betrayal

Before I had a voice, words landed, penetrated
into the marrow. *Defect. Deformity. Disorder.*
The spinal fusion operations were failed successes.
        As in, my vertebrae were determined, no matter

what straightness I desired, to be bent, their own peculiar
version of upright. It's difficult, fused, to turn
        around, look behind myself. I am trying not to take this
as a metaphor. I need to perform surgery on these words,

to sing a song of exhaustion, strip back
        the humiliation as eyes glance, then gaze
beyond, or, worse yet, render me completely
invisible, not only by age, or gender, but infirmity.

I extend my hand-cane hybrid towards the ground
in front of me like a diviner – this path,
this body, not the only crooked things. I mean,
        look, I could trip and plunge

into the hollow of myself, distracted
by this noise in my ears – *if you have a go,*
        you will get a go. What about the unpicked
threads of the safety net? And who are these people

simply watching as we fall? I am trying not
        to take this as a metaphor. We yearn for the
possibilities of another city, another body as we
fall, knee-first onto the blunt fact

of queer promise. We pick gravel out
of pitted flesh, and the ruination of these bodies
leaves us roaming where we are, persistent
        inhabitants of a breaking country.

Andy Jackson & Bron Bateman

Rage: Waiting at the end of crip childhood

Children grow up. When they don't, it's a tragedy. We do everything we can to make sure children grow up, in this strange world of forward motion. We grow and learn the extent of our bodies, and there are whole books on shin splints and first loves and burgeoning existential dread. Children become adults, for good and ill and inevitable.

Crip children usually become crip adults. We keep telling our medical systems this, but the message tends to dissolve on contact. I know I did, but my shout must be lost in the massive stacks of yellowing paperwork that never left the ruins of Melbourne's old Children's Hospital. It is lost in between the expiration of funding at sixteen and unaffordable physiotherapy at thirty. The startled horror when I see myself in motion and realise that, yes, this is as good as it is going to get and *no one told me*, because child medical intervention is all about normalisation and if they just tried one more time and I stretched just that little bit harder then perhaps I could be what they wanted. The good crip child, slipping sweetly and seamlessly into abled life. Instead, I'm left with a comically blasé approach to general anaesthesia, eight falls a week, and the lingering certainty that I have failed capitalism.

I want to catch myself in motion and just see my body, neutral, instead of wrestling with a grief that should not belong to me. Crip children are so often told how lucky we are – lucky to be alive, lucky to receive treatment, lucky to not be as badly off as others like and unlike us. We compete for funding. For patience. For pathos. It is impossible, when the transition from childhood to adult medical services is as abrupt and unprepared for us as it can be, for it not to feel like this 'luck' is some sort of precious resource, and that it is running out. The future of health needs to know the taste and strength of this grief and understand that there is a crip adult waiting at the end of countless crip childhoods.

We are lucky and unlucky, and we exist. Vivid and confused and ever-changing. We are good *and* ill and inevitable.

Kit Kavanagh-Ryan

how do we protect the mutant from annihilation by the 'normal'

a sloth-slow strength stretches like lines of longitude / *sighing*
through my lingering life and other lives before / *oh above*
and parallel to mine gently curving / *a fierce kink in*
meridians of knowledge / *systems fixated on fixes*
without a north / *still our limbs think*
or south / *our minds reach*
outward / unplans
into fractal / ever-shifting maps
brokenness / surveyed by genetic engineers
glittering in the face / searching for repeat palindromes
of maskless eugenicists / about thirty letters long each side
this double-helix of fragility / of the midpoint a snip here
and genius a twisted ladder draws us up / a snip
we wake up into our / there
bodies / deformed
deviant / *real*
dirty unworthy of / *the earth*
life laughter curiosity / *calling to us from*
clandestine desire what we've been / *our wounds*
what we are to become / *a promise against being*
erased / *we ghost the agencies and clinics*
who defines / *revolting in our flux*
our suffering / *this new*
illness / *abnormal*
wellness / *we are*
custodians / continuous realms
of blemish all this / our power as bruised
endangered infinite / and sweet as a persimmon
entangled for the helix there is no outside and no other

Gaele Sobott & Andy Jackson

Rage: Mind the Gap

I've experienced states of ill health since I was in the womb, since I was born, as a toddler, as a teenager, as a middle-aged and older woman. Over time, I've developed a layered consciousness of my aches and pains, my crookedness and a deep understanding of my health. I'm an organic database of all kinds of information on the workings of my body. A researcher's dream. An archive ripe for exploration. Any doctor worth their salt would eagerly tap into my vast knowledge, but doctors don't. I have symptoms of undiagnosed, probably autoimmune-related manifestations of illness that have worsened significantly over the last year. Doctors ask the same old questions, concentrating on the same narrow range of risk factors. They tend to focus on genetic determinants. They fetishise my body parts, my organs, breaking me into smaller and smaller pieces. I bounce from one specialist to another. The gaps between specialisations fascinate me.

The spaces outside the body systems delineated by Western medicine must hold many answers to the cause and treatment of my symptoms. However, more research is required, and doctors are not trained to venture into these spaces. They are not prepared to zoom outwards to investigate our relationships to environments, geographies and histories. They shy away from considering what effect particulate-matter pollution may have on our bodies, the role of ancestry, intergenerational trauma, land theft, racist policing, damp rooms, and heat-trap suburbs. How these kinds of factors interact with our genetics, physiology and epigenetics to impact our health. Neither are they trained to listen. Really listen.

I imagine a future where we keep the best of what works in Western medicine but transformatively analyse and restructure its dehumanising, toxic aspects. We will do away with existing medical hierarchies and elites, racism, and underlying eugenic perspectives. It will be a future where we reconnect to traditional ways of knowing that link us to the earth and non-human life. There will be an emphasis on training integrative, general physicians. Medical professionals will come from varied backgrounds, including disabled, working class and First Nations. They'll unite in their desire to engage in radical struggles for a better world. Medical storytellers skilled at researching communal grief and our place in the web of life will inform diagnoses. It will be a future where science and knowledge are not profit-driven.

Gaele Sobott

Auto-Astronomy

Every constellation is imaginary
and real. Consider
these memories as sparks
of distant light

I am a map with points; separate
parts of my selves. To connect
them, I draw, keeping non-linear,
spherical, spiralled

From out of my body,
a small, shaky voice sings
that classic lyric of men –
O Lord please don't
let me be understood

Medical trauma is created
by those who do not listen

2006, my first date –
at the night's end, I blurt
out how nice it was hanging out –
I may as well have shoved my heart
into the nearby undergrowth

2019, my first ever date –
I am in my 30s. Wanting
to find my person. To connect.
To love, be loved. I am ghosted
like my memory from 2011

1992, eyelids clasped in prayer,
a thin tear hesitating at the lid,
as I think of a saviour –
pale, otherworldly –
as if he was listening
and would lift me out of here

2020, staring at the electric menorah
on my second hospitalisation
better than Valium

1986, my soft hand
in a kitchen drawer, the serrated
edge of the cling-wrap box
slices a wound into my finger –
suddenly, a swoon – I wake
on the floor, my mother overhead

Sometimes I find half-moon
crescents in my skin.
I am unaware of gripping fingernails
into my body until I see the marks

So that's the shape they make,
these flaring points
against the dark oblivion –
a man, running
on the spot

a woman, screaming on the ward
as her mind unravels and her memory
is taken. Charted coordinates
on this complex, moving,
sparking map

Andy Jackson & Anna Jacobson

Branches

wrens nest in keloid branches, feet tiny and curled, feathers bright
my body eats certainty and spits out the bones
        my selves and I, we live outside it
who would want reminders of the things it has endured?

my body eats certainty and spits out the bones
protection blooms through my self-preservation
        who would want reminders of the things it has endured?
I lock inside myself, transforming my mask to a shield

protection blooms through my self-preservation
my body lets the bath unclasp its crooked beauty
        I lock inside myself, transforming my mask to a shield
why do I choose to be here and not in the forest?

my body lets the bath unclasp its crooked beauty
my thinning skin barely blankets a desire to see the world
        why do I choose to be here and not in the forest?
trees are safe, they don't force you to do things you don't want to

my thinning skin barely blankets a desire to see the world
my selves and I, we live outside it
        trees are safe, they don't force you to do things you don't want to
wrens nest in keloid branches, feet tiny and curled, feathers bright

Kit Kavanagh-Ryan, Sarah Stivens, Leah Robertson,
Beau Windon, Jess Kapuscinski-Evans and Angela Costi
(arr. Andy Jackson)

Blurry

Anxiety wasn't in my vocabulary at three years old,
the concrete flight of stairs to our fifth-floor home
still haunting me into adulthood. Then later,
teachers said I didn't write my letters within the lines,
and the pounding headaches, the spinning room, the vomit
on the classroom floor. Between wails and sobs
from a small room with a bed, I heard my teachers
outside the door ask why my parents would send me to school
in such a condition. How I handled those years is an enigma,
a pair of eyeglasses with lenses thick as soda bottle bottoms
the solution. The stairs, my school – suddenly, the world.

CB Mako (distilled by Heather Taylor-Johnson)

The shamed body addresses its owner

I did not ask to be given to you
already broken, bits rattling in the box.

There was no kintsukuroi craftsman
to lovingly mend me with gold
in the seventies.

At two, my inability to catch
presaged much. At fifteen, the hard smack
of my body on the orange lino confirmed it.

I failed to leave home to backpack.
At nineteen, it took my mother
to pull a jumper over my head.
I bought plastic cutlery – not as painful to lift.

In the nineties, real women
wore power suits, did step aerobics
and made up their minds to get over cancer.
Running boardrooms, they ran away from me.

So what could you talk to your friends about,
what was the argot?
You became angry.
To fail was shame, and I sickened you.
You gaslit me, disavowed me. So I waited:
you couldn't live without me.

Make what you will of this febrile pile
stacked as delicately as pine needles

fallen in wind. Do not admonish me
for what I am or cannot be. I am yours to keep,
a broken song, quiet evisceration.

As a baby, I screamed at touch. At seventeen, could no
longer run without my legs veering from their sockets,
like startled birds.

I failed to pass in the adult world but
at nineteen, my voice was a siren song,
passport, justification for being. But the music was not
mine – and so heavy to lift.

Newly woman, I was beautiful, did not know it.
I wore many costumes. On stage people flocked to hear
my song – so startling in its
sonorous tones, caramel density.

Making the sound that others demanded
felt like choking.
Shame made me a trick pony on parade
pacing, pacing until my hooves shattered.
Shame is a heavy rider.
Silence, our disavowed song.

You dressed me to look like the others.
Weekend at Bernie's
seemed funny at the time. People said
I looked like Nicole Kidman, had a bright future.
We both knew better.

It was only at night, when all was still,
that we would write poems together.

And now, your daughter diagnosed,
you speak me back into being,
apply like honey to wounds
language to each deficit.

You speak my names: but will you introduce me
to your friends? Are you still ashamed –

Mother dressed me as she dressed herself.
A funny little simulacrum in white.
People said, "So talented"…
"Exceptional!" Inside,
protest pushed up like needles

through my pores – it was only at night
that I sensed some terrifying possibility

that there might be a song
that might belong to us, some singular garment; not
hand-me-down
not annex to my mother's deficit.

enough to sing it? Or are you still –

Esther Ottaway and Rachael Wenona Guy

Selections of Memory from Double Pneumonia / Selections of Memory from the Psych Ward

I arrive in hospital and once I set foot in the room, I will be there for eight days and eight nights. I will not see my family until the seventh day, and only then because I am having a severely traumatised response. I have become difficult.

In the hospital foyer she read me my rights, tiny smirk at the corner of her mouth. Thumbing the notes on her clipboard she says "It's all here, avoidant personality, somatization, anxiety, obsessive-compulsive disorder."

Stunned, I am bundled off to the psych ward where I will spend four weeks. All I know is that I have been in unexplained excruciating pain since taking a recently prescribed medication. Now I am assumed to be mad.

Some phrases that are directed at me:
"Are you still here?"
"Mind over matter"
"Have you tried yoga?" (at 2 am when a night nurse came in to take my stats)
"Pyjama Paralysis"
"We need to get on the same page"
"I'm not here to talk about that"

Some phrases that are said to me:
"Listen to the language you are using – you've clearly been Googling."
"Well you had us all fooled for a while – we thought you were sick but it's all in your head"
"I told you to desist from manifesting this pain!"
"You don't seem mad, what are you doing in here?"

I wonder what's been said or written about me to invoke these interactions. After the standard number of recovery days, people are different with me. Ninety percent of the time they seem annoyed or suspicious. The medical staff only seem to look in when I'm lying down, never when I'm doing sad little laps of my grey room to try and reinflate my lungs. I start to leave the door closed. I'm trying so hard. I have never felt so tired.

For four weeks I am under constant supervision, must ask permission for every move, earn sufficient trust to be allowed to walk outside in sunlight. My phone and laptop are taken. There are 15-minute checks all through the night to make sure I have not strung myself up. I hear the nurses coming, the clatter of doors row by row by row – my thin stream of sleep broken again, again. I sleep like a prey animal, one eye open.

Vegetables and fruit are added to my meals when a nurse I know in a different context advocates for me. I know that food is a key part of my personal wellbeing – its presence grips on to my energy levels and takes them up or down. The beige reheated slop devoid of nutrients leads to me feeling like beige reheated slop in human form. There is a bag of fruit and some carbonated water left at reception for me by a friend, and when I eat a banana I can feel my cells holding on for dear life to the sunny song of the potassium. It marches through my bloodstream, bolstering and encouraging some movement among the ranks. I source these basic building blocks while I can barely make it to the bathroom and back without oxygen from a nasal tube tethered to the wall.

I hunker down for the duration, shuffle in slippers and mint green, hospital issue pjs in a thick blizzard of benzos. I queue for plastic trays of inedible grey mush and individually wrapped plastic cutlery that is so soft it bends with the force of buttering bread. Still a patient manages to cut off her thumb with one during my stay. Each night she works at it in secret. She says, "please don't tell – I must have one over them." Mornings I sit with her at breakfast, see the bloodied seepage on her bandage, say nothing.

"You have diabetes." A statement – not a question. I don't have diabetes, and I never have. Everyone who possibly can gets my blood checked to find the sneaky hiding markers that prove their suspicions – this fat person is unhealthy and now because of their bad behaviour we can prove it. But I don't have diabetes, although the physiotherapist who entered my room decided that I must after laying eyes on my juicy frame, not my chart.

The lie that landed me here sounds so obvious now. The GP said, "You go to the hospital and I'll let them know you are coming for a special blood test." Of course, when I got there I was promptly sectioned, locked in a small fluro-lit room, read my rights… For a whole month I shut up. I am very polite, I am calm with the psychiatrists. I swallow some bitter pills. I bite my tongue; endure the humiliation of being told over and over I am not the objective judge of my own experience.

"Good girl," she says when I confirm that I've been doing my pulmonary physiotherapy, blowing bubbles with a long, thick straw. A hot flush goes through me, a forty-one-year-old person built like a tank. Good girl? I don't say anything, and by the time I gather all the shards of myself together into a person who can self-advocate, she's left the room. Everyone is always in a hurry.

Well done! You're ready to go home! When I am finally discharged, I am sent home with a patient survey form, tea in a polystyrene cup and a newfound brokenness. I have learned that you survive this medical system by pretending, going along. You crawl deep inside some cavern of yourself and wait it out like a wounded animal.

I won't accept that this is the only way things can be, so here is my hopeful reimagining:
When I arrive at the place where I'll recover, we talk until we reach a shared understanding. I am respected as a person who has lived in this body for forty-one years. The people caring for me do so after listening, not after walking in and making decisions born of a prejudicial gaze. Humility, respect and collaboration are abundant. I am believed.

It is not my habit to hope.
It has taken me two years to regain the feeling in my limbs – yet I am getting better. I am regaining my footing in the world. I am not who I was before, and I still am not sure of the validity of my own story after the experience of being told my story was pathological.

There are green leafy plants in my room. There are comfortable places to sit that don't crinkle with the plastic beneath and there are natural fibres on my bed. There is a bowl of fruit which is constantly replenished. I feel safe and know there are no missing pieces of information. Whenever someone comes into my room, they knock first.

I have been working with an amazing, unorthodox counsellor. She regards me as a whole person, holds the threads of my story as well as my bodily experience with gentle, astute care. She does not patronize me or dismiss my pain; has helped me identify and foster my own resilience, helped me reclaim some dignity…

I join forces with the people around me to see how we can shift my situation in a positive direction. Everyone who interacts with me understands why it's important to get my pronouns right.

All I can do is wait and quietly hum the pieces of myself back together in the presence of friends, in the presence of nature.

There is humanity in every collaboration. My file shares my name, my pronouns, who my family is, the things I like to eat, the words or attitudes that are best avoided – because wellbeing is the aim here.

Each day I plant something for the bees, spread a little seed for the birds, sit beneath a tree, breathe.

There is a deep and collective understanding here that everyone is different. My body takes its time in a different way to most, and things take the time they take.

Jasper Peach & Rachael Wenona Guy

Afterword

Almost five years have passed since the hospitalisation I describe in my collaborative work with Jasper Peach – and I feel impelled to say something more.

In 2023 I was finally diagnosed with an FND (functional neurological disorder). My diagnosis made sense, and yet no sense at all – because culturally and medically we have inadequate language for educating patients.

FND is a poorly understood condition that slips "through the great divide between neurology and psychiatry…" (FND Australia Support Services Inc.) Because there are no discernible biological origins for FND it is classed as a *psychosomatic* disorder. The diagnostic language used to describe this condition harms patients because of the inherited cultural biases around what 'psychosomatic' means. People with these disorders experience debilitating physiological changes because of changes triggered in the brain. Their disabilities are *real* and yet the language used to describe them suggests otherwise.

Language is important. Words shape how we embody illness, agency, recovery or go on to develop chronic disability. We are only just beginning to develop a language delicate and robust enough to hold the complexity of these ambiguous, multifactorial conditions that fall outside of the usual diagnostic guidelines. Language can be a condemnation or a liberation; the difference between feeling further marginalised, blamed for your own suffering, or having the key to empowerment, better therapeutic relationships and efficacious self-management.

As Irish neurologist Suzanne O'Sullivan says "… the Western biological approach falls short [in] making people better... If medical paradigms … are not working, then doctors must stand back and listen to the story the symptoms are telling. The most graceful solutions arise when doctors and patients find common ground."

There is reason to be hopeful – we are currently at the beginning of a paradigm shift around how we understand, interpret, find words for the mind/body conundrum in all its complexity and subtlety.

Extraordinary research in the fields of neuroplasticity, trauma and the biopsychosocial sphere are leading to a different model of understanding about the origins of illness and wellness. New knowledge generates new discourses that shed light on our old paradigms. Acknowledging that the greater context of our lives, our stories, histories, cultures, and the language we use to describe them, shapes our very matter and functioning as we move through life. New perspectives and revised language lend subtlety and a depth of understanding to health care. I have only just begun to sense that I personally, and we societally, may be on the cusp of a much more compassionate, holistic, and empowering view of health.

Rachael Wenona Guy

Uncertain Parts

In my notebook, I record you each in different
colours, hoping this will help me work out who is
saying what, and then why you are saying it. You
are not audible; I perceive you each like a thought.
Some of you brusque and unmistakeable. Others
needing stillness and intricate mental work.

I do not know how many of you formed. Your
existence has come to make sense to me, but my
awareness unsettles you. You have long gone
unobserved. You suggest I have made all this up, or
that I have not and I am insane. You do not have
full access to my intellect nor what I have learned. I
do not have full access to your memories.

Other core facets of identity are challenged. I am gay
and settled in this, but this certainty clouds
when those of you who learned young to please
men get worried I'm not doing so. Others see
danger in an alternative. You fight to my forefront
and rotate your versions of our politics and age and
interests and direction. You flood with your
emotion and manoeuvre my body.
I scramble for ownership.

My psychiatrist notes that I am here more
frequently. These instances are a sharp spring day.
In the safety of these sessions I refer to us as us. I
am to have compassion for you, and to grieve
alongside you. I am to thank you for protecting me
and to help you understand that
the threats have now subsided.

Your threats have now subsided.
My neurosurgeon explains that as I've grown
older so have you. You don't push against my
spine like you used to. No more spearing my
back and legs. Still, you don't give up, like a
bully. Sniping my left foot. Denying me sleep.
You're supposed to be subtle, like regret.

I'm told to monitor you. Monitor. A word that con-
torts my brain into a knot. I know there's at
least twelve of you in me, but not exactly where
and what you're up to and if you intend to get
nasty. One thing I've done is observe if any of
you dare to bulge. Some of you have, like you
want to spring out of me. My skin has been good,
holding onto you, but for how long?

You may remember, two of you had to be
removed. Do you miss them? Do you visit the
hole they've left behind? Were you close like
siblings or estranged like siblings? Do you blame
me for their death? I hope not. I tried to keep
them, but they were destructive. You know how
much codeine methadone and morphine I took to
live with them. I hate surgery as much as you do.

For too long I've compared you to weeds, worse
still, I've written about you as landmines. But I
don't want the responsibility of a gardener or the
fear of a soldier. For over fifty years you sit as I
sit, you eat as I eat, you dream as I dream, when
I'm cold so are you, when I sweat you are hot.
We share this body. This tangled mess of thistles
and thorns. An imploding grenade of screams.
This body we share as a team of uncertain parts. I
hope you can love my body when I can't.

Trees

Trees are magic. We are all taught this as children but then we are encouraged to forget. Red, green, yellow, brown. Big or small they are magic. I, on the other hand, never stopped believing. More than that, the importance of trees is not a belief, it is a fact. Some of the dead brown leaves pile out on the side of the footpath deliciously crunching under my wheels. The old one that must be protected and the new ones that must be given space to grove. There is a tree in a park near the house where I used to live which is like a large umbrella. Its branches hang almost to the ground. If you sit under it when it's full of leaves you can almost pretend that the rest of the world doesn't exist.

at first it was a pleasant warmth
discussing hope with trees
the land can live with bruising

I have been visiting her since I was a child and I would endeavour to visit her until I go back to the earth. Trees are safe. They do not shut or force you to do things you don't want to. They are not violent. Unless perhaps a gust of wind blows one of the umbrella tree "branches" and slaps you in the face.

after the week of angry fire
charred branches point upward
deep inside a bud will wake

But even there there is more of a kiss. Or it is true you could be unfortunate, and a tree could fall on your car or your house. But that is just one of mother earth's ways of trying to reclaim her dignity. Nature is sacred. All green things help to ease the constant pain in my brain. Yes it is true that this happens to nearly align with what the medical experts say is good for anxiety, depression and a host of other illnesses. The process of defending trees' right to exist is one of the things that literally gets me out of bed in the morning.

black-pawed but sitting strong
a koala waits for their supper
the tree kisses embers to sleep

Jess Kapuscinski-Evans & Angela Costi

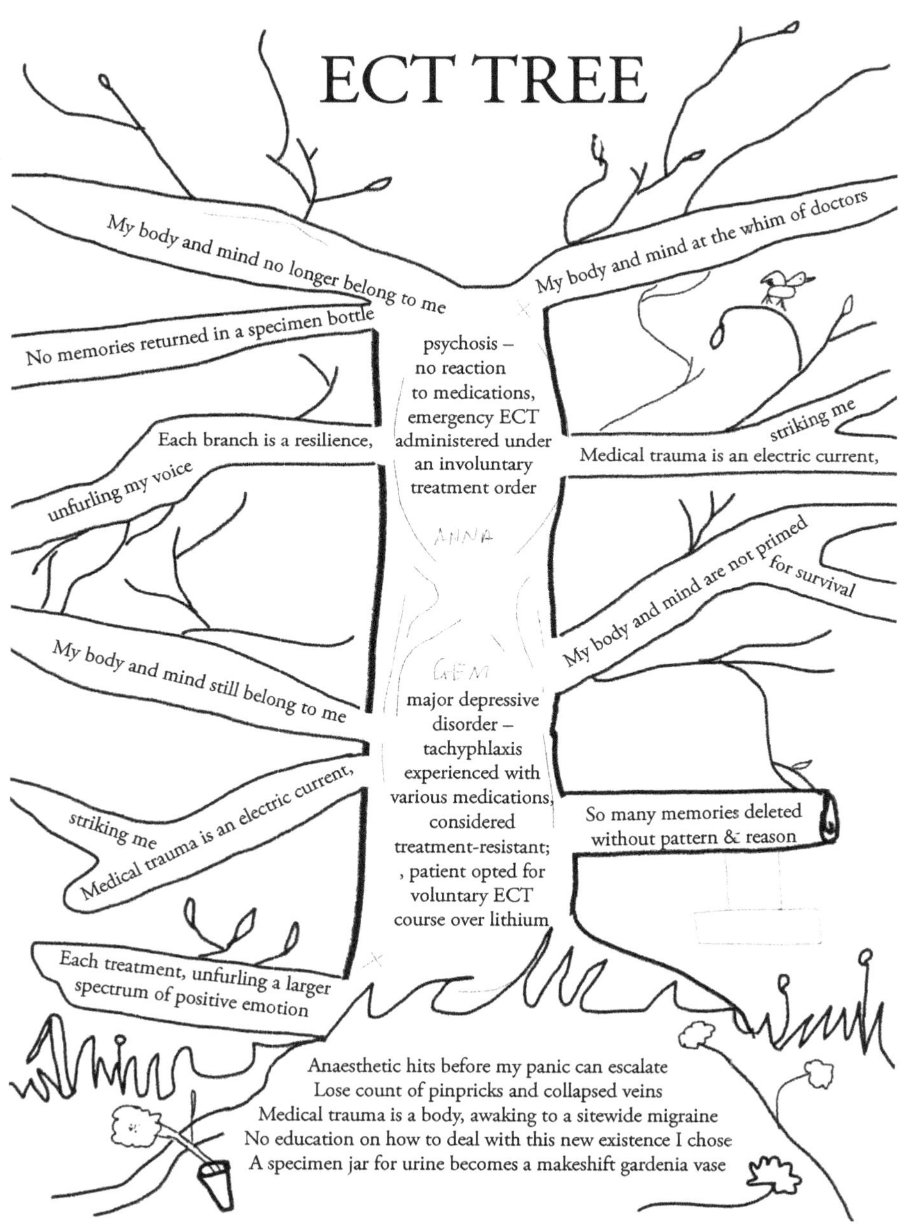

Anna Jacobson & Gemma Mahadeo

Pensive Air: An essay in two voices

I see an advertisement for an estate sale. There's a photo of personal items laid out on a table, and I notice a tortoiseshell comb. A memory: the soft bristles and painted shell back of my Yiayia's hairbrush. How I would watch her as a child, still in bed, as she brushed and hair-sprayed at her vanity. I wonder where that brush is now.

Something about this image of the comb makes me want to close my eyes from the sadness of it. Does this make sense? It feels too lonely that these are the things we leave behind. Something we rely on each day then becomes discarded, unlikely to find another home. Maybe I'm noticing the loneliness of things because now I'm surrounded by the same few objects. My belongings (who belongs to who?) build the routine of a day contained in my home. I brush my hair, empty the dishwasher, place bread in the grill – somehow always managing to dust ash on my knuckles – and think of what it is to live a life contained.

[ ]

They don't appear on the news anymore, even as numbers. More have died these last four months than in the past two years. It's mild. Nothing to be afraid of. They had underlying conditions. They. Ever since my teenage years, I've had to breathe deeply, steel myself, if only for a moment, before opening the front door, stepping out into public space. The way some people look at me. Particularly men. Not that it's life-threatening. Just a long fatigue, a wince in the mirror. Something always pushes me outside. A kniving pain down my thigh reminds me to walk. The autumn sun, alluring beyond the front porch, wants to caress my eyelids. A friend texts, it's been too long, coffee? I'm startled, briefly, to be an image in his mind.

[ ]

I Google 'recluse', trying to pinpoint what is normal. What is healthy. Although I know myself to be neither of those things. I read about Emily Dickinson. As recluse. But also: baker. She would lower baskets of gingerbread out her back window and into the hands of neighbourhood children. I imagine the rope brushing against her palms. Laughter in her face.

I sit with her story. Thinking of my own hours writing out recipes. Watching dough form as the stand mixer whirrs. I pick zucchini from the garden, my dogs circling me as my knees become encrusted with dirt. I grate the zucchini and squeeze out its moisture over the sink. Add it to bread. For my partner, my parents. I turn a loaf out of the pan and onto my black Kmart wire rack, feeling the heat of it and thinking of all the ways I'm connected.

[ ]

Home is familiarity. The risk, though, is not the breeding of contempt. More like a gradual impairment of the heart, a numbing. So I am determined to carve out a place in my bedroom for grief as well as rest.

In a small chestnut-coloured frame, on a low cupboard near the door, I have two photos. One is of my father as a young man; the other, my mother as a child. He died when I was two. She died when I was forty-eight. I see them every day, when I wake in the morning, rubbing the sleep-grit and solitude from my eyes, when I wander over to my bookshelf, and out of the corner of my eye when I watch the magpies warbling outside my window.

After you've had a brief period of mourning, people expect you to keep the bewilderment, shock and ache to yourself. Back to work. Back to routine. Back to small talk. Grief doesn't ever disappear, nor should it. Grief wrestles with the mundane, and they make an uneasy truce. Together, they honour the dead.

A few months ago, I decided to place a small vase in front of these photos, and to keep flowers grown in the garden in it. Paper daisies. Roses. Chrysanthemums. When they begin to wilt, I know it's time to replace them. They remind me of where I have come from, where I am going. I think of ashes and humus. Pollen and rain.

I rest in this room, soft and human.

[ ]

I go through a box of loose photos with Mum. I'd asked her to show me. I wanted to frame some; hang them in my home as little connections to the past.

Some photos are a hundred years old. Mum inherited them from Yiayia and I recognise her handwriting on the back. *31st May 1959*. I look at photos of Yiayia as a child in the 1940s, black and white with rosy cheeks. The added colour makes the photo seem unreal.

Mum picks out small square photos swept with amber light.

'The orange ones are Rhodes,' she says. The island where my family comes from, where some still live.

Moving away from the box, Mum takes out an album. Pointing out child-me. I remember my clothes. The yellow Roxy t-shirt. Board shorts that covered my knees. Shyness radiates through the images. I struggle to pinpoint the feeling of inhabiting that body.

I wonder why it is so much easier to look at my family than myself. I take home a few photos. Ones that were taken decades before I was born. I imagine them in my home. Placed in op-shop frames. Objects of the past, memories of family dotting my walls.

[ ]

> They shut me up in Prose –
> As when a little Girl
> They put me in the Closet –
> Because they liked me "still" –

There's a difference between confinement and reclusion, between being shut up and choosing it. One door has a lock on the outside; the other, on the inside.

Emily Dickinson writes – in poetry, of course – that "they shut [her] up in Prose". Well, here we are, too. In prose. In our rooms, with our photos and mirrors.

When the pandemic began, there seemed to be a collective gasp as people realised that shutting ourselves away could be an act of love. Solidarity through distancing, not in spite of it. But this was not a new strategy. Those of us whose bodies confound our society's definition of normal – who get stared at, who get overwhelmed – have always retreated, to breathe a more pensive air, to write and to imagine.

At the end of the poem, Dickinson writes, "Himself has but to will / And easy as a Star / Look down upon Captivity – / And laugh – No more have I – ".

Surely I'm not fooling myself in those moments when, looking into the shrine I've made, it seems to expand to fill the room? When this body feels like enough? When I sense on my skin the wing-beats and tremors of the world?

[ ]

When the pandemic began, Mum made pancakes. I poured maple syrup and felt the love that came from her making them gluten free, vegan for my partner and with wheat and dairy for Dad. In those months, I knitted, shaved my head, Zoomed. I kept living in a way an awful lot like before. But removed from existing among crowds, without forcing myself into the fluorescent lights of supermarkets, my illness receded. People asked me how I was – and, while terrified, – I was no longer experiencing seizures.

I heard the talk about missing events and replied that I've never been to so many book launches. Now, they were online; I could be there. Even when I was so sick I couldn't leave bed and kept a bottle of Advil in my pocket, I could hear other people's voices. My camera was off, but I was still there. Listening.

When the pandemic continued – and continued – the doors started to shut. I was alone in a new way. I could not leave the house, but now people didn't understand why. Events shifted to in-person, and I could no longer listen. I felt the gap widening.

I used to watch YouTube videos of people walking. Moving through cities I couldn't visit. I wanted to see something different. I would relish living in someone else's world for minutes at a time. Now, the videos have changed: people visit galleries; shop; eat indoors. No masks. I can't watch; it is no longer a comfort.

[ ]

The questions won't go away, pacing the halls of my body like stubborn, addled ghosts. What is normal? What is healthy?

The more time I spend online, working or scrolling, the more I feel a cautious, cerebral aspect of me expand. I curate myself, tuck the complicated emotions into serifs, hovering somewhere overhead. Each word, each click, a decision. This is helpful, in some small way – I inch towards other thoughtful, marginalised people – while it also reduces me.

Sometimes when I leave the house, the footpath can feel like an acutely unfashionable catwalk. Inhabiting a body that is atypical – for me, because of spinal curvature – is a kind of magnet for surreptitious staring or intrusive questions. It's as if I take up too much space. So, yes, sometimes I would rather be reduced.

I ration out my exposure. I meet a friend for coffee, sit outside with them, try to listen without restlessness, speak without thinking too much. Let things float up onto the surface of my skin. Allow myself to be seen.

Katerina Bryant & Andy Jackson

Grace: The Unplanned

Before the pandemic, I kept lists. I would watch productivity videos in bed and imagine how I could shape my future, one dot point at a time. I wrote pages of notes during medical appointments; read journal articles in my spare time. If I was organised enough, I could learn past my body. The future was always on my mind. What will I become? How will I achieve beyond the constraints of illness?

When the pandemic came, for the first time, I cancelled plans. The only future I looked towards was when COVID would end, and, as that hope faded, I stopped thinking of the future at all. I did not feel freer; I felt nothing. I tried to sit in the sun. Tend to the garden. Go for walks. I met people outdoors, and when winter came, I felt the pain of no one wanting to meet in the cold. I said *sorry! I understand! Next time!*

I learnt that thinking of the future became an accumulation of small things: strawberry biscuits in the next Coles delivery; adding 80s horror movies to my watchlist; taking my meds. I stopped worrying about how I would survive this illness year after year. Instead, I sat in the unplanned – the unknown – and waited.

Katerina Bryant

Objects of Illness / Recovery: An Alternating Collaborative Essay

As rainwater seeped through the laminate flooring, I piled my objects onto my bed: an antique out-of-tune Zither, my books, a woven rainbow rug that had made my room my home. I lost none of these objects, but I did lose my shelving, which drank up water through its base. I also lost my room at the rental that had housed all my things – the doorway warped with water damage and was no longer safe to inhabit. I stayed with a friend for two-and-a-half weeks while I tried to find a new place to live. My objects were splayed across three different suburbs, and I felt fractured: one part at the old share house – safe if the disintegrating ship of the bed could hold, another part in the suitcase at my friend's house, and a third split lifeline to my parents' home. I wore my hamsa ring – silver hand with larimar stone eye at its centre – to ward off the evil eye. I needed spiritual protection, wanted to feel safe.

I placed a shell box on my bedside table in my friend's spare room. The top had faded from one ocean hue to another from the tracking sun: Caribbean to Emerald. This box hid all my meds in their blister pack foil, a pill cutter, a dragonfly pill box. The tiny studio I managed to get a lease for wouldn't fit any of my objects. It didn't have room for a bookshelf or bedside table, so I stored five books on a single pantry shelf, my shell box on top. Furnishings and practical vessels would now become my world: my doona cover with its colourful flowering cacti design, my ceramic fruit bowl glazed with the leaves of a plum tree, my purple kettle. I could not bear to part with my other belongings, so I stored my life in boxes at my parents' home, in my old room.

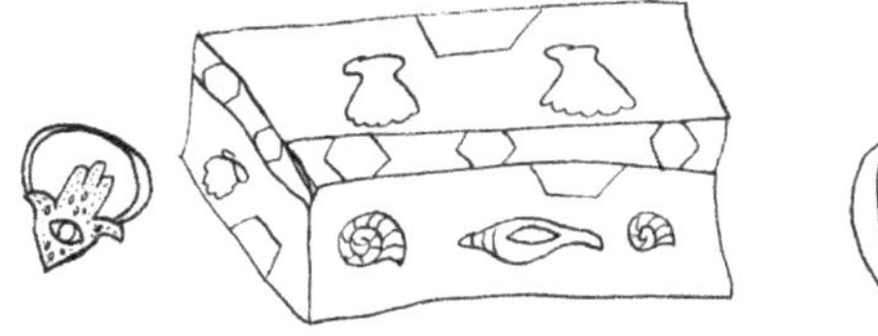

Dad decides to clean the storage unit; he fills his car with plastic tubs, and I drag them into his house. Mum and I realise the boxes haven't been touched for almost twenty years. I expected to find old toys but instead I'm met with a time capsule of the ordinary: worn sneakers, Roxy tee shirts and board shorts printed with hibiscus. Mum thinks it's a mistake that we kept these things. We must have mixed up the boxes meant for the bin. But I doubt it;

I remember how I was as a child. So fixed on objects, unable to throw them away. I would hold on to slips of paper, broken plastic. I once tried to trace this obsession to illness. Was this part of the OCD? But I've since given up this questioning; there's no use in tracking through the past with a medical magnifying glass.

In one box, I find a Winnie the Pooh jewellery box. It's musical and when opened, Winnie spins. His outline is reflected in a silver plastic mirror. The box is empty, except for a tube of fake blood. I laugh, knowing that this would have been precious to me. I've always been drawn to the macabre. In another box, I find clothes. Worn fabric heavy with memory. I take the stack of clothes home, wash them, try them on. I find, with surprise, clothes I wore at ten still fit. It's a shock but not wholly unexpected. I've been more unwell than usual this past year and for the first time in my life, unintentionally lost a lot of weight. I put on a Big W denim mini skirt, with lace edging and a leather cord tie. It scares me how easily I can slip into my child-self; how illness made this possible.

I had long dispersed of my rattling spaceship asthma spacer and the blue nebuliser machine from my childhood. I hated that nebuliser and mask; the droplets of moisture that clung to my face underneath it as I inhaled the muggy vials of medicine like a science experiment. Throwing out these objects felt good. I didn't want them in my sight ever again. I still carried Ventolin in my bag just in case but hadn't needed it in years. My asthma flared on day two of isolation. I had managed to avoid Covid until the third wave, and now slept with my Ventolin inhaler on the pillow next to me. In the morning, the pharmacist in my street delivered a preventative inhaler to my door that my GP had recommended. But I couldn't twist the lid off the device, either anticlockwise or clockwise. I felt weak. I tried for five full minutes, stopping only when a blood blister bloomed between my thumb and pointer finger.

I needed to take the medicine – it was in my hands, and I couldn't access it. I had never felt so helpless and on my own. I called the chemist, who asked me if I had trouble opening jars. I had once bruised my hands trying to open a jar of salsa. *Turn the inhaler upside down and twist so you have a better grip. We'll stay on the phone with you, we'll be here the whole way*. Finally, the lid gave way to a twist. The chemist cheered and I heard the counter staff clapping. I hung up, used the inhaler, and had an allergic reaction. My breathing worsened, and I needed to use Ventolin again. The lid hadn't wanted to come off the inhaler for a reason. My body was rebelling against the asthma medication. My body didn't want to be that ill child again.

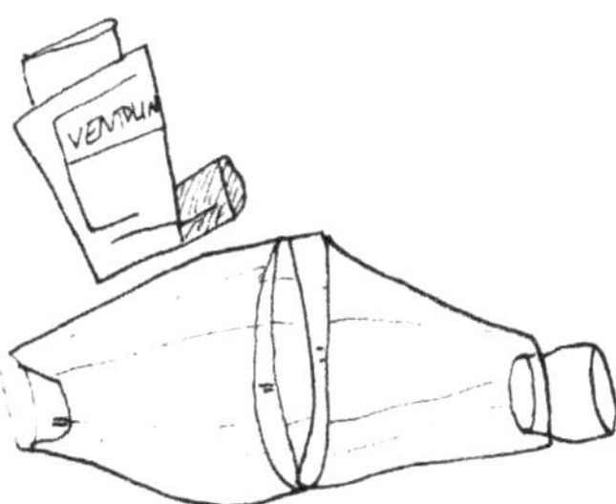

If you asked, I would say I wasn't a sick kid. In my story, illness came – heavy and thick – when I was a teenager. At fifteen, I spent three months in bed. One illness coming after another. I remember loading *SVU* DVDs into a chunky laptop. Time slowed, measured by discs. Around that time, a friend called me on my Nokia. I had a bad fever, and my words didn't make sense. Later, she asked if I remembered what I said; I didn't remember that she called.

Now, approaching my thirties, I realise that this story I've built for myself isn't quite right. Illness goes back as far as my memories do. At seven, I synced my breaths with the counting that repeated in my mind. I was terrified; if I fell out of rhythm, something horrible would happen. I would go to bed, padding around the house in dog-covered pyjamas and checking all the light switches. Once, and then again. In case my mind was playing tricks.

I remember thinking this was the way everyone's mind works, but I wonder if – even then, so young – I was lying to myself. I hid rituals, kept thoughts unspoken. Secrecy felt natural. Perhaps I knew I couldn't be understood.

I couldn't be understood by others, but my unconscious mind knows me too well – my dreaming mind. When I am ill, my dreams take me on massive quests. Sometimes I feel better on waking, as though my body has found a way to repair through the night. Sometimes objects are given to me in dreams: pieces from Escher-like staircases, balustrades crumbling in my hands. After this dream, I wake with my hands clenched and sore, move them to get rid of the stiffness. I am in my thirties and beginning to feel pain. I don't want to tune in to my body or I will feel more pain. In another dream I am standing on the foundation stone of a house made from Paddle Pop sticks. The walls are lifting; the house is empty. I am still living in the tiny studio I found during the floods, my belongings at my parents' home. I want to be surrounded by my things again. But nothing will fit.

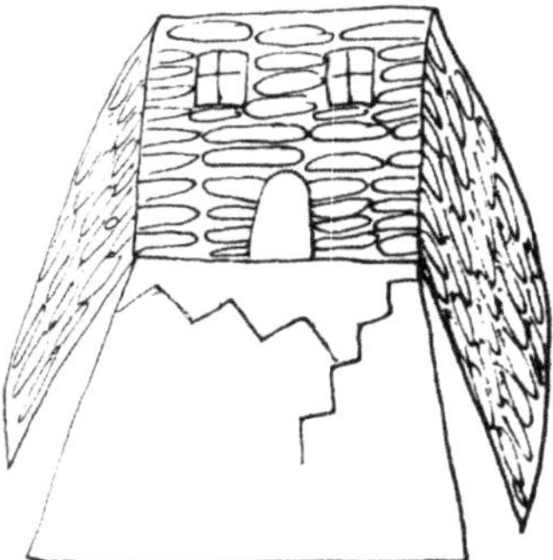

I dream I'm in high school, walking the same path from lockers to class; class to lockers. It's not an uncommon dream for me, and lately there's a new addition: I am told that I didn't *actually* graduate and must go back and do it all again. From this I wake, sometimes damp, and think about the power of objects and place. I remember the thick blue carpet of the English classroom. The toilet cubicles where I once closed the door so hard, I broke it and locked myself in. I couldn't bring myself to crawl under the door. Maintenance had to be called.

It takes months to realise I'm dreaming of a place that no longer exists. Of folders and plastic slips that were long ago abandoned to landfill. That part of the school has since been renovated. It's not the only place that exists in my dreams. In sleep, I go back to my Yiayia's home. Now demolished, but while I'm asleep, it's as it once was. I see the daisy bush, covered in bees. The garden is unchanged, and I listen to the windchimes, bright in the afternoon breeze.

Objects and places hold strong memories. For me, when I'm well, the kitchen is where I can be creative. I buy a cooking pot at Lifeline to boil pasta for one. There's something about its shape and size that I like. At this Lifeline shop, there's a whole kitchen section with everything from jar openers to egg slicers. I buy the jar opener for $2. When I am well, I cook and bake. My current rental doesn't have an oven and the one hotplate that works is temperamental. But still I manage to make kimchi fried rice with egg and coriander. Cooking is a sign I am well and have energy again. I can sense when the oil is hot enough, give the ingredients my care. I choose my own patterned tea towels, serve my food in painted bowls bought long ago from either Target or Kmart.

When I got out of a psychiatric hospital in 2011, after psychosis, the first thing I made at my parents' home was potato gnocchi. When I got out of a psychiatric hospital in 2020, after an antidepressant changeover, the only thing I could manage to put together was a peanut butter and banana sandwich. Meds can make me very unwell, and I have had adverse reactions to the majority I've been prescribed; some have nearly killed me. Food is different. Often, it's one of my only joys. A well-seasoned dish filled with flavour and good ingredients can make me cry with the first few bites.

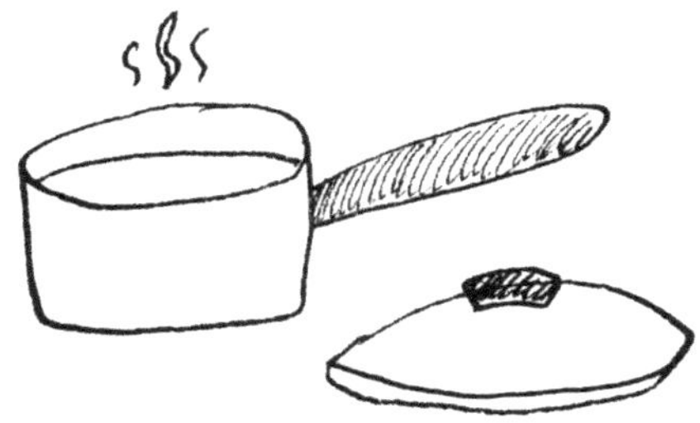

When I can't sleep, I imagine myself entering my home. I open the door and list each object I see. A wooden chair with a woven leather seat. A bargain from a store I drove past after a haircut. A framed watercolour from Vinnies. Coat hooks bought off Facebook Marketplace. In my mind, I form the objects I see every day. The act of imagining them and where they've come from – now united in my home – is peacefully mundane. I move through the house, checking off each item, until sleep comes.

Before the pandemic, at night I would visualise packing a bag for a trip. My hands would fold clothes into perfect squares. I would leave with not too much, nor too little. For years, I fell asleep to the idea of being perfectly prepared. Not until writing this do I realise the peace I find in the presence of objects. It's a flimsy calm; things break, are repaired, or ruined. Yet, there's something about objects that settles me. This feeling comes, too, when walking through a museum or op shop. Perhaps it's the calm that comes from looking. When I focus on what is in front of me, I am taken away from what is felt within my body.

Anna Jacobson and Katerina Bryant
Illustrations by Anna Jacobson

Debris

Innate badness is the cause. Language of
abomination. Witches vampires whores dogs

imagery of filth. I am filled with black slime,
open my mouth it will pour out. Assure child

they are not at fault. Refuse to be absolved
of blame. Considerable achievements, none

to her credit. No one can truly know her, she
would be shunned, reviled. Angry male gods,

whatever is required of her. Nidus of
dissociated alter personalities.

In his bone marrow, a choir chants its earworm
medleys. Some part of him can't stop singing along,

hearing *stare* as *blade, being seen* as *judgement.*
There's no rewinding the tape back before names,

no transplant for this hurt. It's not enough to know
that when he recites the lyrics out loud, they

sound ridiculous. He wishes he could hear
differently. Maybe then, he could be in the body

that is loved, find the subliminal rhymes.
Broken as open. Other as wisdom.

Leah Robertson & Andy Jackson

Left column, by Leah, is an erasure poem
from Judith Herman's book Trauma and Recovery, chapter 5.3 "Child Abuse: A Double Self"

Crack and Burn

My brain tells me it's as good as wet bird shit
on the driveway and this time, I don't believe it.
It's not used to the rebellion; normally I smile politely
as it wreaks its havoc.

My trauma therapist tells me I am deserving of kindness. My cruel and clever
brain says (in a voice indistinguishable from truth) if that were the case, I would know
how to be without despising myself. I nod and they both smile back.

There are so many ways to make the intrusions look like quirks
if you're creative enough. I've never met a friend I wasn't afraid of
poisoning. They say I'm the most detail-oriented, attentive
dinner host they've ever met. The cheese can go back in the fridge.
The cheese can go back in the fridge. No one will die if you put the cheese back in the fridge.
Good, the cheese is in the bin.

In the seventeen years since winning the criplotto it's been so easy to make friends
and rather hard to keep them. I don't show up to their events, help them move or look
after their kids. The generosity I can demonstrate hinges on deep listening, connecting
them to others and being a sounding board for rearranging thought. In the honeymoon phase
they'll bring a meal over when I'm sick. The novelty wanes once they notice I'm sick all the time,
or they expect my body to change and accommodate something it can't. I can't.
We stay at arm's length or sever ties. It is a drifting or a door softly shut.

My brain tells me I am mere minutes away from dying
and this time, I don't believe it. Behind every bouncing leg is a panic attack
waiting for the starter pistol to fire. There's a pain in my chest.
There's a pain in my chest, my left arm, my leg. There's a pain in my chest,
my left arm, my leg, and if I'm lucky I'll just faint instead.

My body keeps being my body and my mind meanders
through thoughts of what will happen when I die. I want my ashes split
between the garden at home, Gantheaume Point, Sisters Beach, and the dunes at Somers.
I don't want social media to be awash with grainy photographs from that one time
I was in the same place as someone, performative connection clogging the feed and building
a false frenzy. I think a lot about the dragging of time, the glimpses of goodness often marred
by the pain it takes to be part of things. I keep trying to learn how to rest.

I've always had a body that wanted to consume itself.
Invisible pain means imaginary means suck it up means faking.
The doctor writes "too young for that" in the notes on their computer but no
other part of me gets the memo. Sometimes it's a welcome distraction
from deciding which contagious disease I have this week.

I've always had a body that found it excruciating to carry the frequency and volume of feeling,
of wanting. There is an echo chamber in my brain that makes my connective tissue crack
and burn, and a heart that leaps and soars from one stepping stone of sky-high joy to another,
never finding the sweet spot. Never at rest. Waiting for the other shoe to drop from the sky
that's falling.

My brain tells me I destroy everything I touch
and this time, I don't believe it. There are others
with minds like mine. I found them on Instagram
while I was trying to dissociate and now, I have my own ammunition.

There are vast and jagged swathes of my brain that tell me I'm making it up, cruelly
describing the waste, the lack of gratitude, the salty snippy complaints I share so wilfully, making
a mess everywhere with my thoughts. I chip away at learning to care for myself and build a team
to scaffold and support my terribly nervous nervous system. This body that won't keep up,
or upright for long. Even when morphine doesn't dint the pain, I doubt that it's real.
I learned this from the medical system, but before that, I learned it everywhere
through every sense, each detected mood giving clearer instruction than (wholly absent)
direct communication.

There are patterns, this isn't something that only happens
in my shower or when I don't get enough sleep. Different bodies
with the same fears, different aches with the same stories.
Our brains tell us that we're alone, but we know not to believe them.

When I look at you – all of you in this otherworld for the lost and magic word whispering godlike
goldhearts – I'm not too much. I am not someone that doesn't fit and I am more than the sum
of my unending insecurity and litany of aches.
When we gather in these numbers it's impossible to feel less than because all I see
– everywhere I look – is raging grace and powerful repose.

Sarah Stivens & Jasper Peach

Kissing Gates

In the before my heart lived to serve
and I made it my business to check
what they thought, why they thought it
where they placed themselves in relation
to me before I could locate my stance.

Yes. I do need to reduce my pain.
Ok. I will buy what needs to be bought.
You're right, I am terribly broken.
Mmm, weekly attendance would be wise.
All of it so loud and trampling and tall.
Looking down at this body I handed over.

Tremendous harm befalls the one that fights
not enough or too much, the impossible tightrope
of being good and kind and fair and loving, first
to others then to yourself. I got it so wrong.
To be a burden to anyone is the most
destructive havoc I could imagine.

Then in the quiet, quiet, quiet
of work dried up,
appointments cancelled,
my body my body my body
it whispered so calmly, so certain and still:
Your name can be something that fits, just for you.

In the quiet, my body left to stiffen and crack
to find its own rhythm bereft of manipulation
no helping hands to iron out the creases
as I curled into myself I could hear what I had always known.
Not a proper woman, definitely not a man,
terribly (wonderfully) broken and big and loving.

I gave away the clothes that felt like grief.
Found a new therapist who came with me
as I turned over all the stones at my own pace
tried on one name, then another,
and when I found it, unflinching and right,
playful and shimmering like my core in the stillness.

Pain is here, and gripping tentacles of anxiety
marching beneath my skin in that moment before
the hollow nest of sleep arrives for the night
again and again. It's nothing to turn away from
or cure or change. When I listen and let it be
there is a glistening lake of strength and surrender.

I have passed through the kissing gates, nudging
up against one another in parallel, at prayer,
and found my peace. Letting all the fight out
and through, looking at my reflected image in water.
I always thought it would drown me in an instant,
but it's here that I can look myself in the eye.

There is great purpose in pain
then ego dictates an attack on our personhood –
turns away from notions of harnessing its power.
That a sensation can befall a man of strength,
we can only do away with it – call it weak,
broken, damaged, insufficient, out of balance.

We are lightworkers of pain and love, the baritone
of it a grounding hum that echoes from the soles
of our feet and resonates through the sky and beyond.
If hell is suffering for eternity, what name could we give
to being in our bodies when the song it sings is jagged
and cold, hurting and real?

My heart made it out of the wreckage somehow.
It was painful to locate the missing pieces,
quiescent defect, the quiet bloom of the unfurling aorta.
Before I knew the particulars I didn't feel the weight of it.

Yes, I am terribly broken, but that's ok:
I will sit with the pain, I will do what needs to be done,
I will contort myself into the necessary shapes.
Ok. I will devote myself to this new occupation of illness,
of wellness. I'll relearn the routes, map out my world anew.

Well, it's accessible, there's just a couple of steps to get there.
Well, it's accessible, but I'll need to be carried sometimes.
I'll raise hell when I need to, rest when I need to.
I will be too much or not enough.
Then in the contours of my new life
I'll reimagine myself, embrace what's left
and what's next.

Look at this body I built! What a mess,
this beautiful disaster. It's a wonder
it hasn't keeled over yet. Look,
I've sharpened the edges now, I've honed myself
against the whetstone. I've flung myself against the wall.
I've fought for all of it, made peace with what I've got.

I renamed myself for birds and asteroids, seeking flight
and freedom. I'll be soft. I'll be rock solid. I'll keep going
til I keel over. Reject the impulse to apologise for the mess
of survival. Spit fire at anyone who thinks it's tiresome
to give a shit about each other. If I'm to be a burden
I'll be Sisyphus, I'll take my lot
and keep rolling up that bloody hill.

Sometimes I'll still find myself
weeping at the wrong end of dawn
when pain keeps me from sleeping. Ok,
I'll stay hydrated. The body needs catharsis
to clarify itself. In the quiet of my body
I'll learn a new rhythm.

The gates open up before me,
one after another. I am opening
into myself. If suffering is a crucible
I'll reforge myself from hellfire.

Jasper Peach & Robin M Eames

Questing Beast

Michèle Saint-Yves & Robin M Eames

Questing Beast

1. CEREBRUM PISCIS

/bɹeɪn/, from *brægen,*
perhaps from **bhragno*:
something broken

You know   it's there though you can't see it in plain sight
You know it's there   you have one it's plain to see
It lurks in a cortical cathedral
lurks in a plaster-cast skull
among gelatinous matter
amongst plastic dendritic fronds
living a double life
living as a sideshow alley prize
waiting for subconscious currents
awaiting subterranean springs
both held by backbone
both born/e in fluid
this Ulyssean species
this Amphibian.
And yet   I,
I   am dry.
Swim to me, swim to me
silver slivers quickening
along the axiomatic axons
across the synaptic void
breach the spectral surface

2. CERVIX OLOR

/swɒn/, from *$swonh_2$-/*$swenh_2$- :
to sound, to sing

Her neck arches like a swan's,
sometimes advancing, sometimes retreating.
At first glance it seems too fragile
to support that monumental head,
perhaps a dozen cervical vertebrae
concealed in the improbable length,
armoured in glittering scales.
The cognitive load is immense.
Every now and then the creature
lashes out in anger or hunger,
then relaxing, then turning to preen
the fiery mane trailing down
the monster's flexible spine.
Sometimes she calls out mournfully
and from that gentle throat expels
the sound of thirty questing hounds
howling in pursuit, chasing an end
without end: seeking answers,
seeking care.

3. CRIP VOX

/ ˈstɔː.ɹi/, from *historia*, from ἵστωρ:
to see, to know

Release your valves
Flare your gills
Raise your hackled fins
Scar me with your cranial cæsarean
swim to me, swim to me
Swallow the Earth at my three-toed feet
Drink the clouds abutting my horny head
Bite the sun out of my draculian heart
Suck the fire from my reptilian belly
swim to me, swim to me
Waiting to let you unfold me
Drown me in your amnioses
Saturate me to the marrow
Produce my sorrow
Swim to me, by this old cold white light.

4. SCAPULARUM AEQUĀLIS

/ ˈfɛð.ɚ /, from _*péth$_{2}$r̥,_ from _feþer_, from _fear_:
a feather, a pen

The howl echoes across cityscapes,
fuelled by a noxious volume of polluted air
gusting out from powerful lungs,
cradled by a writhing knot of ligature
(the æ of chimæra): a huge and artificial suture
replacing what might have been ligaments, tendons,
tender swathes of connective tissue.
Somewhere around her raised hackles
the scales fade into leopardlike fur,
a mantle of stained gold and bronze.
The shoulderblades wing outward into feathers,
each swordlike quill sharpened at the tip
to slice through misdirection. These weapons
often turn against their host:
her back a tattered mess of blood and bone.
Somewhere in the wings a surgeon prepares
to enter the operating theatre. Soon
the lights will change, music swelling
as the performance shifts between acts.

5. CRYPTHAND

/ˌɛt.ɪˈmɒl.ə.d͡ʒi/, from etymologia,
from ἔτυμον & λόγος:
truth of words

PRO- fess
ST- ress
HE- ro
TIC toe

LIM- pets
B- eats
S ates

APP- lic ant
AR- tic ulate
IT- ali cised
ION is ed

GH- oul ish
OS- cill ate
T rol led

MIR- ed
RO- rt
R apt{e}

MICRO-biome
PRO- teome
CESS-pit
OR bit

ELEC-tric
TRO- pes
DES tiny

NEU- ro logy
TRA- ff ic
LI- ght en
TY ran ny

CIR- cus
CU- nt
IT ch

SH- it tier
OR- ph aned
T en/or sion

AMPule of high or ultimate relief, grief of loss of LIMBo land of purgatory, purging so as not to die, lied to about light weight ARMament from the stockpiled artificial armery, amoury a concept as lovers ABANDONed me hook line and buckle strapping my elm vessel to the helm of my scared and scarred stump or stem, as what is left of the branched tree CHOPped, chippered to imagine a whole me, an AMPutee, a ghost of that which could reach to the sky, lying rooted, connecting to the mycelium metro polis, underground ministries administering a circular route to health, well, being well in my ordinary matter of life.

6. VESTIGIUM

/ ˈmanstɚ /, from *mōnstrum*, from *moneō*:
to remind, warn, foretell
a divine omen, a marvel, a miracle
a deformation

At the conclusion of the creature's
awful spine, her leonine haunches vibrate
with hidden tension: at rest but never
resting, only pausing until the pursuit
begins again. Always chasing a quarry
that can never be caught. Always spinning
in endless beautiful movement, whirling
in chaotic rotations around a centre
defying definition. She waits, she chases,
she waits. Her predatory hips obscure
the prey beneath, her rabbit-soft feet
gentle, unlike the rest of her. She waits.
She chases. Stars flash past her as she
picks up speed, driven onward by lithium ion
and something else: a powerful nucleus
of fierce love, solidarity, survival. At the end
of her story she will not be cured or tamed.
She will transform again into a different
kind of monster, brave and dangerous,
forged by struggle into a pure and glowing shape
whose contours cannot be mapped.
She writes the rest herself:
the story starts again.

Michèle Saint-Yves & Robin M Eames

Rage: Therapeutic Future – ReQuesting the Beast

The two genes SMARCB1 and LZTR are applauded for their lack of vigilance. No longer chastised or worse demoralised for their inability to stop the Schwannomas. *Let the tumours grow* we say. Let them become part of the intricate thread weave sequence of nerves sheaths blood and bones of life to be lived without the *dis*. The dis is no longer a point of reference. Recall how we did away with the word *abnormal*. We tended to say, a *concerning abnormality* in our notes. Now the dis is no longer useful. A disparaging dis is dissuaded from causing disease disability disingenuous discourse. We are at ease with your ability to generate these intricate stops and starts across the terrain of your remarkable body. Teach us your pain and we will listen.

Angela Costi

DALY (Dragon-Adjusted Life Years)

If dragons **exist**, then surely, **I can**
be more than the forms that ask
if I can reach my arms behind my head
or whether my mate's eyes are likely
to **grow** back in the next six months.
if **we can dismantle a world** in fiction
and shape it into cloudseas
and world trees, the big made small
and tiny turned huge, our fey laughter
tasting of silver and lost music, our
skin gone to scale and tendons split
for wings and our bones hollowing
into flutes for this new wind
and all the fire we swallow and share,
then what about **crip futures**? Can we—

—we make all that and more, but I ache
with **the** part of me that shapes our **magic**
only into **cures and curses**. The part
that knows **only** to **imagine worlds**
where, if magic dared to reach
any of its filaments into my brain
or my eyeless friend's bone
and socket, **chaining together**
what was never there
until he **bloomed** sclera
from new soil and nerves made
marvellous ropes of themselves
and **the brain knew the light**
was let in—I imagine ***magic like that***—
and how Centrelink would ask for **his whole**
life back in recompense, down to .5 cents.

I fear **what we would do** with magic when
the world should be thick and full of eyeless dragons.
Flightless dragons. Wyrms **with** spastic wings
and tail amputations and fiercely palsied
faces, bones brittle and the **fire turned inward**.
We live scolios-spined and mad and clawing
into our palaces of rock that smooths to
the coils and curls **of our** furnace **bodies**.
Magic is in the architecture that **lets us** crawl
on our mighty bellies—in the **trust** it takes
to fall from the sky. There should be dragons
who gleam with bright prosthetics, melted down
and **remade** to fit us **as we grow**. Let **our**
faultlines murmur until they roar. Let
us burn anyone who dares price our scales.
I want to be left **glorious**, overstretched.
Pleased **and soft** all at once
nestled in the bones of those who only died
supported **and** strong and **safe**.

Dragons exist.

I exist, I can
be more if I
grow.
We can dismantle a world
and shape it into
crip futures.
The magic
cures and curses only
imagine worlds
chaining together
what
bloomed
from new soil and nerves.
The brain knew the light.
Magic like that—
his whole
life back.
What we would do
with
fire turned inward.
We live
in our palaces
of our bodies.
Magic lets us
trust
fall,
remade as we grow. Our
faultlines roar.
I want to be glorious,
and soft
nestled
and safe.

Jasper Peach & Kit Kavanagh-Ryan

Rage: *Meta*critic Oath

We know this one well: "its core premise is to give the participant their own power and control away from a centralised experience".

We've been told this a million times: "system's infrastructure allows users to own their own data, secure their identity and privacy, and control content."

We have heard this one before too: "You will essentially be shareholders, not only having stake in the capital but benefiting from the economic and social dividends it provides."

The Web3 premise built on Blockchain infrastructure integrated with NFTs and cryptocurrencies, leveraged on public governance ledgers such as copyright protections, will enable the Internet of Things (IoT) to be freed from its shackles. Anonymously.

Wearing VR headsets, it will be as simple as a patient based in [India] and a medical scientist based in [Australia] having a client consult inside a virtual reality metaverse. They complete the consultation using their crypto wallets linked to their metaverse accounts. The course of medical treatment is the patient allowing the scientist access to their unique blockchain node of their DNA for their particular mutancy (a digital string of their GCATs), the scientist onlining the CRISPR machine to edit the genebotic code and instantaneously signal cobotics to clone the new code and inject into the patient's aberrant site to replace mutated cells with perfectly healthy replicating ones.

In this process, the scientist is simultaneously linked to biobanks and discovers the patient has a unique DNA mutation that is found to repel certain viruses and they leverage a copyright protections contract from the governance public ledger, anonymously. They then have a virtual meeting with a medical research lab and sell the now 'their' DNA as NFT to that lab anonymously, receiving payment through a leveraged sales contract from the corporate public ledger using cryptocurrency.

Welcome to the world of AI generated shamanic avatars and mail order manifestations, where your GCAT and 01010101 straddle the helical flux of the next gen matrix.

A matrix of tokens, of divid(e)ends that is chained by block[heads], replete with fungi, trading in cryp[t]s, with a great deal at stake.

Michèle Saint-Yves

Touch some grass

Touch some grass and other phrases
thrown at invalids and Soulslike players
who quiet too loudly – *don't*
be too sensitive, she said. *You're so*
– I want to take the words between my teeth,
show the iridescent mothwing bruising
in traces that you leave behind.
Your body touches mine
and I can taste it in my throat
while you talk to me
about your new fandom until
you're hoarse and *is it too much?*
It's too much, I'm being –
– I *want* you to. I want you and
all your echoes, laid out. A dragon's hoard
only willing and shared.
It takes time to lay this body down
(grass is further away than ableds think)
but I want to, with you, because
we are exquisite and we can crip
this time. Together
and parallel.
You are enough.

Thinking about touch as a way of telling
grass from astroturf, earth from the inhuman
world, I press my ear to the murmurs
of my insides. I'm not cold, I'm just
unlearning what a crawlspace manhood can be,
how far from the surface I am, burrowing
towards you with a mouthful of dirt.
All I've ever wanted is your
touch, to unhear *misshapen*, to hear
beautiful and not shrug it off.
Your body sings its lament of caprice,
hums courage into my mouth. Tell me
all your crepuscular truths,
give me your soft kisses that dissolve
this shell, then press in seeds of *more, more*.
It takes time for grass to push
blades up through these self-despising
myths (green shoots, fine hairs, hard to see
some days) so I want your rain, to
be rain for you. To speak, to listen,
as our vast, cumulus
bodies open.
We deserve this.

Kit Kavanagh-Ryan & Andy Jackson

Stealth Mode

Stealth mode: I am the biggest person in the room (in a roly-poly way,
in a medication-wrought-sleepy-ravenous-default way, it keeps me alive
and giant). I know my body exists in places and that I am erased from perception –
I don't look the way we are told over and over from every direction
that bodies are meant to look.

I am the most twisted person in the room (no, not like that, I mean literally,
spine like a shaken disused staircase, or a tree trunk bent by a ceaseless wind).
I wear a kind of invisible confidence-armour, then people remind me
my body is there – my self, buried underneath the idea
of how bodies are meant to look.

I know I take up more space than most, and that people are stunned
to collide with someone they didn't have any idea was there. My name
called, I take a moment before stepping up to the microphone home. This is
a place I know how to work, how to bend and throw the soundwaves out
to other bodies. I tell the truth as best I can in ways that haven't been held
in the minds of those listening in the moment.

In crowded spaces, people brush past me, assuming my body is a regular
shape, look acutely awkward as they bump into the curve of me.
If I wanted to be safe, I would hide, and I have, but I keep stepping up
to microphones, stages, footpaths. What am I doing here,
acting as if their eyes on me couldn't hurt? This is the only way
to approach that quiet truth none of us have quite absorbed yet.

It's impossible to underestimate a person you didn't register
as human or as even being really there. But what
I've come to understand – with all this scraping work
of heaving myself out from underneath structures that
erase and control all of me – is that this is a blinding light,
and they are moths that bump up against me.

I am underestimated, overestimated, misestimated.
There are stories people tell themselves about me,
stories that contort how I'm seen. Tragic, pained, heroic,
flickers of monsters and saints. Yesterday, I caught sight
of the knotted bulk of me on a screen
and shuddered – but is this shame or awe?

How to navigate the wanting of high wattage, to stoke those
embers of belief into a warm glow that carries folks into rooms,
shepherds them to the mic, to stand and show who they are?
I've never received attention like this, it's like someone trying
to extract my pulse and eat it, so I protect my breath, say thank you,
let their wanting drift to the floor between us.

It's easy to claim I have buried the seeds of my defiance
in the soil of their gaze, to forget how slow trees grow,
so I may not actually get to eat much of the fruit.
History doesn't make me feel confident.
But having a fused spine means it's hard for me
to turn around, look backward. This is also a metaphor.

If I could whisper feather-light into their ears, "it's ok to know
you deserve a reprieve from hurt", would it help?

What if this was a whisper? These words, flight feathers?
Does this poem contain enough breaks? Enough prosthetics?

I am 42 and my body curves in directions made
by self-protection – I tilt my head to be smaller,
safer – it creates flickers of pain in my skull,
neck, scapula, all along my arm
and into my hands.

I am 51 and not counting any more
the number of times I've wept, withdrawn, soaked
in a warm bath, or been heard and held, or not,
and stepped outside again regardless,
right body in a wrong world.

I am realising this for the first time, and when I notice
how I've dodged a bullet made of sigh-smoked pockets of air,
all I need to say to myself is "be tall". It hurts
to hold my body in a linear way, unmuscled
and unsupported in postures of confidence.
The heartwork is one thing, but the physical – that
may take a few more lifetimes (be tall, be tall, be tall).

I am realising this for the first time again, and again,
standing in the hailstorm of the normal. It's exhausting
to stand my ground, yet sometimes I sense the presence
of other bodies, before, behind and above me,
feel the shelter of their calm, their fury. Then a voice –
my own, and not my own – "you are known, loved,
be here, be here, be here."

Jasper Peach & Andy Jackson

The dysautonomia dialogues

As if my very matter was in argument
with itself – my senses verge on intolerable.

Within this skin everything is on
a spectrum of discomfort –

I smell the fetid underlying nuance
of all things, teeter at the edge of nausea.

My feet throb, recalling the ground,
sound shatters my attention.

Joints drift from sockets, my sternum
quietly unzips itself in the night.

Vertebrae pop and scrape as I mobilise
this assemblage I call my body.

In sunlight the capillaries' high-pitched
howl crackles beneath my cheeks.

Water leaves me burning. Textures
overwhelm.

Sleepless again, the weight of my
body assumes a detestable ache.

I have longed for soft sensorial places
but found no refuge.

My skin winces at contact as if the world
and others in it were to be endured.

Discordant song of my becoming –
are you the kink in my proprioception?

Come night, the heart once again
hammers out its arrhythmic nocturne.

Too little   too much
hot/cold   in/out   heart's thud.

Instead of strength,
this tickertape of error messages.

Hand-addressed distress,
precision pain –

weakness my inherited land.
Trekking the boundaries of quagmire,

how to construct a shelter
in a marsh's connective tissue,

where serpents nest, waterfowl
cry down dissecting nerves,

plovers peck at eyes.
My wetland body, my scant skin

translucent in sunlight, and burning.
Where to make camp

when I slump into seizure,
when friends gently disrobe me

chock my body for the quake?
King's horses, king's men   they couldn't

and can't. Can't – my name –
sleep, wake, eat, stand, breathe,

lust, turn up. I am the friend
whom the kind have given up asking.

And now, cardiac panic shrill in my ears,
my diving bell breached, and filling.

Esther Ottaway & Rachael Wenona Guy

Grace: How's your day?

How's your day? Mine is like this:

I wake up. My cat is waiting to be fed breakfast, and she is the only living creature I know who depends upon me, so I can't let her down. I get up, pull back the curtains, and find slippers and shuffle to the kitchen.

Once I've fed my cat, the other life stuff. I'm already up, out of bed, so immediately, I switch on the kettle for tea. The first cup is always for my day meds, the second, and sometimes third, are for enjoyment of hot drinks generally. Breakfast: granola or toast for breakfast if my hunger has kicked in.

After breakfast, shower or wash, get dressed. Then the day: answering urgent emails, trying to get reading done (ideally for an hour or two), maybe have lunch. Most often not. Cat will be wanting my attention for most of the day. Loads of cups of tea and snacks will be consumed.

Dinnertime comes and I either cook, or eat leftovers from what was cooked a night or two ago. I'll be ravenous by early evening; I'll watch things on my laptop while eating. I'll play my second instrument for a couple of hours. Exhausted afterwards, shower and wash before bed, hot drink with night meds.

What I've written above is the ideal day, week, month. Am I an unreliable narrator? In that I've told you how I *wish* my days would run, and not how they run, more often than not? Do I make excuses for not having my day/week/month be like this regularly? Often an anxiety for those with chronic invisible illnesses.

So, how is your day, really? My day is actually like this:

I wake up to darkness, covered in sweat, though it wasn't particularly hot overnight. My head is hurting. The kind of ache suggesting that it is very late in the day, and that my body needs to have at least one of its antidepressants.

Sometimes I wake up screaming, shouting, fighting whatever perceived threat or danger came about. My mind knows that, but my body takes much longer to register this. A housemate will have fed my cat. She is often next to me, awaiting my conscious presence. She helps me to readjust to the waking world.

I gingerly get up, trying not to upset my balance. Limbs are wobbly after one of these long sleeps. I make a hot drink, take the most essential medications, maybe eat something. My head is thick with fog, or perhaps they are clouds, pregnant with rain. It's dinnertime, the microwave clock will often confirm.

There are two options after this: either stay up and watch fluff on YouTube, take night meds a couple of hours later and go back to bed, or stay up into the night and early morning and skip night meds. A good friend understands the allure of staying up all night. The loneliness of a c-PTSD diagnosis and its symptoms seem more bearable when the other people in the house, the nearby world are asleep. All seems quieter. Some part of the brain equates that with more peace, less threat, safety. Stillness, and less stimuli. Thoughts feel crisper, not weighed down by persistent brain fog.

If up all night, I fall asleep at sunrise, wake up around lunchtime. This tends to break the bad sleep pattern. More often, my brain may need to purge, work through things too confronting to explore in waking life, and will experience nightmares for a few more days. The constant in my ideal day and realistic day is that my cat is never far and at some stage, will always be asleep on me, near me. It's also a reminder that I haven't woken up in hospital.

Gemma Mahadeo

Rage: Living Invisible

The future of health must include research on women, as women are still routinely excluded from many studies, being seen as too variable (or its old term, "hysterical"), and when they are included, findings about women as a group are not analysed. Taking autism as an example, it is not known what the true prevalence of autism is in women, because studies were done on boys, and diagnostic criteria came from those studies. This is typical of all areas of health, as researcher Caroline Criado Perez, in her book, *Invisible Women: Exposing Data Bias in a World Designed For Men*, powerfully documents, and terms "the gender data gap."

This data gap about women is vast: a search on the bookselling site Amazon returns just twenty books on autism in women in the world. Leaders in the field say that women with autism find it as disabling as men do, probably more so, since social expectations of women are higher; but women are usually without the benefit of diagnosis, let alone assistance. They present differently to men, though not that differently: much of the problem with getting women diagnosed lies in a gender stereotype which says that they can't be autistic.

I want to see that change, along with other fields of health research. A 2015 Dutch paper states that "the specific effect on women of a huge number of existing medications is simply not known", yet it is women who are taking 80 percent of all medications being dispensed. Heart attack criteria, such as pain down the left arm, are true only for men, so women more often die undiagnosed. Pacemakers don't work properly for women, since only 4 percent of medical device data studies include women as a sub-group.

Then there is the black-hole data gap of "women's health": menstruation and perimenopause. With no experience, and not much research, to draw on, male doctors are notorious for dismissing and gaslighting girls' often extreme pain and distress in these areas. Australian Professor Sonia Grover, former President of the International Federation of Paediatric and Adolescent Gynaecology, says "If a girl is experiencing pain every month that is stopping her from going to school, playing sports, or enjoying her life, that is not good enough, and that is a condition that needs to be addressed."

I want autism to be diagnosed in women, medications to be trialled on women, heart attack criteria to be accurate for women, pain relief for period and endometrial pain to be made available to women, hormonal therapies to be made available to peri-menopausal women, and women who report symptoms of any kind to be listened to.

Esther Ottaway

References:
Invisible Women: Exposing Data Bias in a World Designed for Men, Caroline Criado-Perez.
https://toopeasinapodcast.com.au/peafessional-gynaecologist-sonia-talks-about-periods-pain-and-managing-them-both-a-lot-better/

Grace: Pleas(e)

When I think of healthcare and what a better future might look like, I come at it from the point of view of a woman living with chronic illness. I come at so many, many things from this point of view, it's true, and now that I'm middle-aged, I am also dealing with an outrage of fluctuating hormones, and I see these states of being as complementary and contradictory, most definitely symbiotic. I want more attention paid to perimenopause and menopause, please, because for some strange reason we've chosen to ignore it. A loud and inclusive discussion of perimenopause and menopause, please. One that involves more research into perimenopause and menopause, with the researchers listening to women dealing with perimenopause and menopause symptoms, and *doctors* listening to women with the symptoms, *please*, and while we're at it I'd like for young females in the beginning stages of their illnesses being made aware by their doctors of what might happen during perimenopause and menopause, because it is all part of long-term planning and management and care. Please? *Please*. I'm trying to be polite.

Heather Taylor-Johnson

Pandemic Year Three

Parent with a headcold,
A child is sneezy.
My nose and ears feel blocked,
And there's that high-pitched buzzing.

Hearing devices ran out of battery,
so did our AAC.
Augmentative
and alternative communication device
Auslan sign language,
Visual Schedulers
Creating Social Stories;
When all combined,
tells a story
Of Hard of Hearing
And bilateral hearing loss

Parent and child
At home, together,
While on the table are
multiple hand sanitisers

It's cold today.
Cloudy and dreary
It's nearly three, time for a nap?
Child signs no,
and wants to draw and
colouring is fun.
We find BTS and BT21
We colour Shooky and Chimmy
while still very sneezy.
Soon it'll be winter and
we're global pandemic Year Three

Chilled through my mind
I weep for a blanket
My thought process is blocked.
And everything feels fuzzy.

Can't talk/text/tell you that I'm out of social battery,
So I don't, I don't.

Creeping through technological devices,
I am lost and voiceless
Vision obscured
Lost in my stories.
When all combined,
I am a confusing story.
Of Hard to Know
And forced self-isolation

I am alone
At home, together on my own,
While on the table are
My cracked hands, hurt but sanitised

I can't leave my bed
Weather too warm
It's nearly thirty degrees, craving a cold wrap.
I miss being a child,
Like when I would draw
And my mum would lie and say it was good.
I just want to GTS
Black out my eyes so I can Go 2 Sleep
while still on my own
Soon I'll be strong but
Forgive myself, it's a global pandemic: Year Three

CB Mako & Beau Windon

Perennially gaslit, the disabled reject humanity

No kerb transition to gentle my chair's fraught crossing.
I wrangle through as I wrangle
daily, scantily resourced, MacGyvering my problems
(no doubt I'm feigning them.)

My employment future: forever 2IC –
power positions for the full-time only
and no more Zoom to reach me in bed:
the pandemic's over now.

Everyone so nosey to know
why-can't-you, demanding
tabloid drama, that I bare my underbelly
and let them test it with a foot. Why aren't we terminal,

easy to process? We fit no system, too weird
or not malformed enough.
Doctors' skeptical stares,
Centrelink's razorlike instruments,

support services too busy to call back.
We aren't wanted,
won't be missed. Little wonder
that we shy now at this pillory

go to the insects, plants, land, sky.

Esther Ottaway

Instructions for the broken

Go to the insects, plants, land, sky.
Turn your phone to silent, your neoliberal
inner critic to vibrate. Take the air.

Approach the soil, where microbes
might temper your clatter and panic.
Let the pardalotes and silver-eyes adjust

to your presence, resume their grazing
on psyllids and larvae. Soon you'll become
only another human, abnormal as anyone else.

Accept, with your pores and fine hair,
the tenderness of the autumn light. Now
lift, gently, the limp body of the magpie

from the asphalt, away from the relentless
traffic. Dig a hole, larger than you'd think.
Push the soil over the body. Release

yourself into weeping, into feathers
and sorrow, decay and rage, worms, bones,
blood, rock, breath, every other thing, here –

Andy Jackson

After writing a book on female autism, I decide to bury it

Go on with that public Esther, curated pretense:
to be and not to be, that is Australian.
What good are these chalk traces around spent victims?
Why lift the sheet on myself, fatigued, confounded?
I know what I'd be next: that bleating woman,
the blaring car alarm that barely registers.
Truth-pregnant, I laboured. Her name is Repercussions.
My fear: that this child kicks, draws breath to cry.

Esther Ottaway

After reading her poem, I remember the diagnosis they give me

Monstrous, so I speak well, as distraction or defense,
but my achilles heal is that I'm mammalian.
What tweezers might extract these brutal dictums?
Isn't this reticence, this fear, well-founded?
Ashamed and proud to have failed as a man,
my flesh holds these undissolveable slurs.
Hunch-drunk, I stagger, assailed by concussions.
No point getting up, this stigma says. In these lines, I try.

Andy Jackson

Raging

I am headed out and one thing I know I'll get (aside from some looks based on my hot pink wheelchair, assistance chihuahua, lab-mask) is angry. Anger is my lipstick lately, hidden behind a fierce mask, because it's where the world has pushed me.

I never thought of myself as a lesser being before the lockdowns. I thought I was disabled. I knew I had one hip higher than the other, one Achilles tendon, an Olympic-level ability to catch germs, and a PhD in pain. But I also have blue eyes, and a big arse and you tend to think of it as the package – the smattering of luck or genetics that gets you to yourself/makes you what you are. Comparison is for products, not people, was my feeling.

The return of face-to-face services and events changed all that. You told me right up to the grille what you thought of me, and everyone like me, who still had to stay home to stay safe. You dropped us in a heartbeat – the Zooms, the remote access sessions, the opportunities to appear via video – from your programs. Why? I asked. Why?

The answer was simple to you but chilling for me.

"I don't like Zooms".

Anger.

I don't like the idea of dying from a virus I can avoid. But don't let that inconvenience you. It's your world, apparently.

The anger of people with disability is different from mainstream rage, I've learned.

Mine is "bad for me". It's unreasonable and for all kinds of reasons.

It's probably a product of my medication. Am I on steroids? Does my brain damage make me frustrated, perhaps that's my problem.

Dwarves, when they are angry, are funny, apparently.
My arse they are.

Or it's the pain, the continual pain I'm in, that's made me the ungrateful, unreasonable witch with a pen who despite being paid to lounge in bed all day and get waited on, wants more. Now she wants to go to things. Now she wants us to all change everything to suit her.

Who does she think she is?

I've added the dislike of Zooms to my list of 'but I can't meet your unreasonable demand to join in' that includes, 'heritage buildings', I'm too expensive, and your suggestion that I make suggestions about how you might fix the problem, because you are very busy with real issues.

Able people issues. That involve people without problems. What is it that's wrong with me anyway, again?

Never mind that most businesses and institutions are still using Zoom for their in-house meetings between colleagues, or that you have no qualms about posting your weekend Netflix (screen) binges on social media.

How about the fact that our careers are at stake? You remember us, the people who aren't programmed because we can't get in the building, without a flying fox propelling us through an upper storey window? Or who need an interpreter to come with us?

And our audiences, who are similarly banging their heads on the floor with frustration – just now quite comprehensively aware that their book-buying dollars and festival presence are surplus to requirements. But I have always maintained that the obverse of anger is fear.

If your audience is only composed of high-value people (no gimps, no oldies, no screens unless you are a super-hot star of a capital city festival) and the program the same, all the more room for those mainstream voices – the echo chamber of homogeneity – white, middle class, university dominated and between the ages of 25 and 55, there should be a good dose of fear for what might be missed; or set aside into silos of tenacious beauty because we are here and we aren't sick of the virtual world at all.

I was talking over FaceTime for a few hours today with another who shares my flavour of disability and we were in escalating peals as we swapped descriptions of our 'getting ready to go out' routines. The research, the planning, booking and funding – incontinence pants and hot packs for pockets – and it all goes too often to a rageful, lonely time in tears at the discovery of two steps others felt you could manage, or the entry bell high up on a wall beyond arm's reach.

Naturally we choose to spare ourselves indignity.

There's a genuine bliss in attendance online, with your own screen dark, relaxed and able to attend to and enjoy the work before you.

Of course, we still gather in the rooms of Zoom, and publish, video; interacting with our International brethren who have retained far more of the advances in accessibility gained during the Covid-19 lockdowns, welcoming a greater reach for artists and products.

what if a new space yawns   between
the rafters   and the joists   spare
air untreated by the chemical decide

comparable of nowhere   jostling
with the   rare

It is the contradictory expectations that set us up to fail.

I tried to be the quiet one and you looked over me. The anger grew.

I tried to be the loud one and you told me I would achieve more if I were quieter. The anger grew.

You built a room with stairs and then pointed out that none of us had turned up. The anger grew.

Then when we did show up, you told us it was up to us to advocate for ourselves. And still, the anger grew.

You put us through the wringer as kids, forcing us to grow up much faster than we should.

Then when our peers eventually grew into adults, we were treated as children, infantilised into a paternalistic punching bag.

You see it in the kids now, their smiles are forced. They're told a path to choose if they want to succeed. But once they get to the summit, they're pushed back down the slide. You tell us to stand straight but to also run and hide.

What's the point of education if we're in our special schools?

What's the point of employment if you won't let us use your tools?

And while I'm at it – "special" – what the hell.

The truth is harsh but we know it means you don't want us near you, it's not that hard to tell.

You look at us and recoil – "thank God I'm not like that…

"I haven't sinned so I'll be right in the universal tit for tat."

You offer us your thoughts and prayers and go home to your cosy Shangri-la.

You vote for tax cuts to buy that new car, then moan about the cost of living.
Let's talk about living. Those taxes funded ours.

Not investing. Not renovating. Not private schooling kids.

Living.

Getting out of bed. Having a shower. Eating. Seeing the sun shine.

When society loses sight of what's important, we've lost our way.

So let's talk about expectations.

We have expectations that you will let us live.

Live the way we want, not at the whim of some carer,

who doesn't want to get vaxxed because they read something on the internet about microchips and Bill Gates or some crap.

You don't just have the luxury of regular meals and warm homes, you have the luxury to think those theories have an ounce of truth.

We're asking you nicely, so politely, to please be a good neighbour.

But this is real, this is it, we don't have a choice.

And you shouldn't either, yet you rub it in our faces with some stupid Facebook post.

So yes, the anger grows.

And when it explodes, we're told to be quiet please, or we'll go to the next in line.

But now I'm saying to you this: 'next' and go far from this dark room.

You don't like mandates? No worries, leave this street, this town, this planet.
I'll see you all on Zoom.

Kerri Shying & Sam Drummond

Rage: Disabled POC

Blunt, we are triple whammy.
Gender. Race. Disability.
Face us,
embrace us,
This is our reality.

To the able-bodied POC
We are not your Model Minority.
You shun us, but we persist.
You give us barest accessibility, begrudgingly.
'Do you want your ten-minute portion – your portion has Auslan?'
No, the whole event inclusive of Auslan.
'Do you want your story in audio?'
Not just my section of your anthology but the whole anthology.
Then silence.

You move on. Move on to the brightest star
The POC who is more beautiful and popular
And in that liminal space
You left us hanging
And yet we persist like a thorn in your side
Sweep us under the carpet: hide them well, don't hand them the mic.
You turn your back on us.
Yet we are still here
While you deny that the pandemic rages on,
We ask for a hybrid session
Online, please.
With captions, please.
With an Auslan interpreter, please.
We would like a Bla(c)k POC Auslan interpreter, please.
We ask politely.
We explain patiently.

But nothing except erasure,
ignoring us purposely.

Our Disabled QBIPOC Collective is slow,
DQC is compassionately slow.
But your deadlines are deadset, unmovable;
Your announcements and timeframes are too short, too fast.
Did you make sure we won't make it, that we won't last?

We purposely wear shirts with the words
'The future is Accessible'
This is the future – the new normal,
You wanted us to 'Live with COVID'
Without pandemic mandates, without required facemasks
Only 'suggestions'
There are 'recommendations'
During the month of Disability Pride
Victoria's active cases and deaths at its highest
But we are here, indoors, at rest.
That's all we can do at best.
One day at a time, we tell ourselves
We'll get through this.
One day at a time is your mantra
Meanwhile, you see people without facemasks on social media.
You cannot fathom how they could be so...
Uncaring?
Unconcerned?
Meh?
POCs gather at an event
My kids' school called for Parent Information night
These events give us all a fright!

Give us food and grocery options with Home Delivery
Give us access with online sessions!

Finally, as I type this,
my child is remote-learning while
waiting for the latest COVID-19 vaccine.

CB Mako

Our Pain, Our Whimsy

We are the blankets curled around each other's ankles in the height of winter. A well-stocked medicine cabinet and a script that arrives at the door without being asked. Without having to remember. A GP who believes everything on the first go and everything after that. Quiet hours at the supermarket where nobody stares, the safe foods always in stock. There is no normal. Hands do what they need to, voices make sounds no one is surprised by. There are enough houses to go around without someone needing to die first. Sensitivity isn't a game to be played— it's how leaders are chosen. They are chosen by us this time. Wheelchairs and stims in parliament. Kirribilli House is now a sensory room. Children wear whatever the fuck they want and no one tells them to sit still. Or how or who to love.

We are free to scoop out life's yolk, jammy and jubilant. We clock off for as long as we need to, prioritising care and comfort. Our trauma matters, our pain, our whimsy, our complete and utter loveliness. No one is denied their needs. No one is denied their humanity. Play is for all ages – to squish and fidget and immerse and create. 'Age appropriate' becomes an anachronism. The veil of maturity, professionalism, toxic positivity crumples to the ground. We are whole; we are held.

Sarah Stivens & Alex Creece

Joy to my world

here is the pleasure   kitty-cat warm
on the sunny winter concrete just inside
the gate me an undelegated inconvenience
luxury thrown out the specialist's window
day one clawed back   this decade living crip

joy to my world

it's not undone   when you go   do your thing
without me a sliver in the heart of compassion
a shard of glass in the regarding eye of country
freedom is your fairytale washed out with tears
melted why don't you join me in the sun

tablecloth ripped out from under
happiness' crockery
never trusted joy
cross-wired with dread
took years untangling the electricals   but now

joy to my world

is my revelation: in life's second half
I'm larking about   letting off
delight's fireworks in cranial sky
jackwiring neurons to sensory bliss
orchestrating razzamatazz

Kerri Shying & Esther Ottaway

Criptych:
Hey there legs eleven

does it feel like plodding   to walk with your two legs
clip-pity-clop horse-foot   envying my glide

heart skipping a beat as you   mind the gap
I transcend   ramping   i'm never afraid

of gum stuck beneath the seat
snail-trails on the sofa   my house

walks

Criptych:
Wheeling the sticky delicious

the wheels on my chair go round and round
round and round
wah wah beep beep beep
gradient too steep   over-turn   heavy door
wack wack scrape twist bash
bruise   the 'Quickie' logo on the back
like an April Fool's note
stuck to my jumper at school
they snigger at the thought   yeah yeah
disabled people don't have sex ha ha
it's 'Karma' (another brand of wheelchair)

unpick the labelling stitch by stitch
i'll decide the naming   the style   the speed
        fast   slow   wet   dry
two or even three in the accessible toilet
        behind the bush   edge of couch
in my bed   in yours
                    whatever   wherever
the mood strikes   modified missionary
        round and round   up and down   mutual
consent   buried soft   lip tip of tongue
moon-ripe   press   heat   wah wah   orgspasms
   double helix rainbows exhale
                                one hell of a ride!

Criptych:
Joyride

Listen I said I'm hell on wheels
burning up the bitumen
I'm that vroom vroom mthrfckr
that TiLite street fighter
that acid green that sleek freak
lean mean meme machine
I'm that speed demon born 2 ride
that deadly sin that crip pride
that battleground that unsound
that rebel yell I'm hellbound
I'm underground I'm thunder
& lightning I'm frightening bipeds
w that BEEPBEEP that tyre shriek
that too fast too young
I'm well hung high-strung

yeah I'm that scream queen
that in-between seize the means
that high risk heart disease
uncomfortable mortality
that eugenic disposability
emergency ward striptease
hospital glam night shift
that fall risk that plot twist
stuck in the hydraulic lift
the grift the grind that grand design
see u on the picket line

I'm circling I'm rapid cycling
I'm that manic panic that
aerodynamic that didactic
that dialectical materialism
that trans contagion that
survival mechanism
that narrative prosthesis
I'm spasticus autisticus
I'm the lunatic the mutant
the monster the mad bitch
the noncompliant bad crip
the fetish fuck the tokenism

yeah I get around I lie down
I'll throw down I'll sing out
WHEELS UP STREETRATS LET'S GO
watch out we're revving engines
we're revolving we're in revolt
hey I said I'm revolutionary
age of devolution baby
I said solidarity not charity
I said rise up bash back

Comrades listen I said
this poem kills fascists
I said sing out ye disenfranchised
wheelchairs of the world unite
the manual the motorised
the rollators the sweet rides
the homefires resistance
the sticks & stones the inpatients
the impatience the invalids
the involuntary high vis

the dole bludger proletariat
the sick cunts the slam dunks
the red flag union hacks
the ticking clock cardiacs
the ethical dilemmas the
queer hypotheticals
inflammatory radicals
the persecuted masses
black armband insurrection
the final retribution

Listen
I said the revolution's coming

Kerri Shying, Gaele Sobott & Robin M Eames

Rage: Invisible (In)divisible

The years of the last decade have seen me slowly become more and more invisible to the general population as I make my way along the street, through the shopping centre or at the movies or theatre; crutches or cane in hand. As I age, my status as a sexual being, my embodiment as a desiring subject as a result of acquired disabilities, both visible and invisible, cast me into the shadowy hinterland of being ignored and no longer valued. No longer am I seen as the vibrant and engaged person of my twenties and thirties, where my status as friend, lover and mother was highly regarded and acutely visible. No longer am I recognised as significant. People audibly huff in annoyance when I move too slowly in front of them. They push past me in an aisle or on the street with little heed for my safety. Children, including my own 4-y-o, ask why I walk like a penguin. My status as a disabled subject denies me agency and cultural significance.

However, I am also a poet who performs her poetry at events around my State. My poetry is frank and often confronting in nature and belies my disabled (or crip) status. As I make my way to the stage on crutches, or with cane, sometimes even in a wheelchair if I am feeling particularly unwell, always seated as I perform, as I cannot stand for long, I see the focused gaze of the audience before I start. Their breaths held in unison. Their eyes turned from mine. Their pity. Their discomfort. Their embarrassment with what they think I will offer. As I begin to read, their expressions change. They start to see me for who I am, the masks and illusions stripped away—a middle-aged woman who is desiring and desirable, despite her physical limitations. Who shares the universalities of love, pain, suffering, sexuality and joy with lovers, family, and friends. Just as they do.

The extended applause I often receive after a performance seems tinged with a collective air of relief, and sometimes a little confusion. I have disarmed these people, made them aware of their own prejudices and confounded their understanding about me and about a crip body in general. I use the term "crip" in preference to "disabled" as I want to confound understandings about what constitutes a differently abled body. I have a great deal of anger and pride in telling my stories and the autobiographical nature of my poetry functions as something that stands up to prejudice and ignorance and says, with a shaken fist held aloft:

I am here. Visible, Queer and Proud, Crip status and all.

Do *not* misunderstand my attitude. Do Not Fuck With Me. With Us.

Everywhere and anywhere. We are legion.

Bron Bateman

Rage: Joy beyond the *futurd*

I have the dirt from my garden fresh on my fingers as I dictate this, planting seedlings into spring beds and neither activity within a cooee of my capacity ten years ago. In thinking of the future *(it typed 'futurd'- now don't be like that)* I have to reference both the chaos and the capacity for deep sustaining changes that brings joy.

Joy is that thing we all want – it grows when the needs a person has are met in the key elements of their lifetime – it's our job to see our fellow's joy can be supported. It took four service people time and energy, and money from my NDIS grant, not to mention the buttressing offered by friendships, to give me back the quiet Sunday morning preparing to grow my own vegies.

What do I think of, in our future, aside from ramps, and food and a house I can live in? It's joy. It's no luxury.

Joy is an orgasm, because there's a particular vibrator that's suitable for a person with my type of vaginal damage, and vulvodynia (which causes painful sensitivity).

Joy is Revlon red nail polish, or close to it, in a low-toxin formula that won't bring on my migraine. Safe food – the cheerful free home delivery from the only Celiac butcher in NSW. The wheelchair bus provider who says 'of course you can bring friends on your social outing', meaning I get to socialise with all my peers, and not in two silos.

Joy is a Zoom meeting, with everything others get available to me too – so I don't have to risk a hospital stay to watch poetry readings or attend a conference. Joy is saying "I'm on the spectrum" and getting the reply "do you have any access needs" instead of "everyone is a little bit" or "no, you aren't, you're so chatty".

I think the future has "butterfly screens" full of people deaf-clapping, with subtitles and new ways of sharing, room for us at protests and festivals and even monetisation of remote access. My future includes bigger thinking than the 'futurd' I'm invited to believe is 'new normal'. That's a futurd of bad practice. I always tell people – I'm living in our future – you are all coming here one day, I just rushed in and got my ticket first.

Kerri Shying

Grace: Inching

Futureproofing health outcomes seems like folly,
a farce. But – when we look behind us the gains
are exquisite. Worked at, pushed into place:
a kneecap reacquainting with its hollow.
This is where the work matters.
I imagine I'll be dust, parts of a bird's nest,
memory and sorrow by then. My absolute
insistence on what is unacceptable to me
being seen, heard, exposed (like a nerve
like my body like my hurts like my fear),
it is inching toward change.
An inch is so much – a piano key, a kindness,
equality and access, understanding, safety.
Even if I don't see it (and I won't), it will be worth it.

Jasper Peach

A History of Resilience: Future Photo Album

after "Imaginary Album or, When We Die, Our Polaroids Speak to Our Living Descendants" by Art25

When the tides wash in under a morning's glittering horizon, our history of resilience will be told and retold over hundreds of years and through tens of thousands of bodies. Who are we? We are parents and siblings, lovers, and friends. We are crip—beautiful things. We are pain and eloquence. Pick at the frayed edges of our narratives with calloused fingers. Be prepared to shed blood, separating salt from iron. Taste it upon our tongues. This is what it means to create a world with words, layer upon layer of truth that lies under a mantle of suffering. Look at us, look. We are more than the sum of our scars. Although we hold trauma in our roots, and it grows, tangling with thought and nerves, it can be tended to grow in strength and joy. We make music with the shells and shale we walk upon with naked feet. We make flowers with the rise and fall of our lungs. We are lions. We roam the world.

Memories finger history.
Bodies braid me. To think,
extricate your tongue from
what is. Regrow from
beneath my voice. Gather
the beautiful to-come.
Claim 'we', a tide of
returning. Unfold into
holding, trust your other.
Scars here see air from
each embrace.

The morning's horizon will
be of bodies. We are lovers,
we crip 'beautiful', 'pain',
narratives separating from
taste. Our tongues create a
world of means. Look more
— scars hold roots and
thought can grow in music
with flowers of our lungs.

We are.
We are
l i o n s.
Returning
for what
is ours.

Bron Bateman & Andy Jackson

Grace: We need what we deserve

Health is as much about each other as it is about ourselves. Our ill health goes far beyond medicine and healthcare services, has nothing to do with BMI or hospital charts. When our most vulnerable people are struggling and isolated, we are not healthy. When our care is segmented into discrete parts – minds, bodies, skin, eyes, teeth, whatever – with varying levels of accessibility and affordability, we are not healthy. When we are simply hoping to survive, not thrive, we are not healthy. When our culture is embedded with ongoing colonial violence and all forms of bigotry, we are not healthy. We need holistic care as a community. We need art groups and inclusive design as much as we need doctors who listen. We need progressive, culturally safe workplaces and service providers as much as we need free medications. We need gender-affirming care as a right, not a privilege. We need universal basic income and universal basic services, not one or the other. We need fun as much as we need rest. We need what we deserve: the very best that life can offer, that we can offer to each other.

Alex Creece

walking document

I take walks after [redacted]—part the air with my projections—///compulsion/// kick through street debris—coke cans—commuter artefacts—wonder if the leaves—regret their falling—must feel good until it doesn't—must feel [redacted]—muster yawn—

sweep the soul of my shoes—check good—check more— thrice the looks carve through my boneheaded fleshbowl—check panic—disregard—am I the bad guy?—my bones crave attention that my body can't crush—leaves leave trees—must [LOST] nice—no don't—they will all see you—me—commuters can't—coked artefacts—fear of regret—

mutter dirt words—enough to feel (swept)—trudge on/up—revive ticket,,, check—yep—sir—understand [gone]—understand [left]—now look at past (passed?) like it's a bite mark—click heels—(and here exploring my capacity for magical thinking… and here considering the parts of trees we rarely get to set our eyes upon… and here I might upend the act)—crisis of ink—

I fear my own dark thoughts—know they are not me—no . . . they are [KNOT] me—I turn myself round in tooth gnashes—sir—you did not expect me to be [gone]—this—this like a—click heels—my name belongs in the dirt—scratch my skin for the ink to deposit—must know—must not—disbelief—what is ([{REAL}])—walk with my diagnosis—regret falling—feel feelings in a #HELPME way—but leave me alone you [redacted]—scream through it softly—

I thought my own dark fears—shaped them ([{REAL}])—I, the searcher—muddled as a playground at dusk—slant as a synonym for loneliness—patient as a waiting room—turning left upon my next omen—trip on a fragment that scratches the itch—I, the cursor—press my arrow to the source—[[[again]]] or {{{through}}}—ever—ever aware of my [minute   ] in relation to God—

The Dem[ ]n is so large in relation to me—I am a fire—hard like heresy through my isolation . . . the cursor drops through—my finger scrolls down and down and down and [[[down]]]—I am down [[[again]]]—falling {{{through}}} my thoughts—won more time—know me as the long blister on the skin of worry_—_splintered and hurt and ready to hurt (COURTESY CALLS me the porcupine)—I don't mean to be a monster—I sting sting sting sing—lalalala—

chorus often—bridge patient—it's time to watch the rodents as they exit—passing mean over debris—(gnashed lichen—lost inklooks—crush synonymous—holy tickets—scratch commuted)—towards::: anywhere—bowling their magic—yawning monstrous—as I know *forward* sometimes has to be::: less (((loving the path)))) more (((rinsing minutes)))—so—so—I think—wait up for me—

Beau Windon & Ruby Hillsmith

Coalescent

Pleading with others has got me nowhere
the gate to my heart is damaged // the gate to my head is gone
fragile is the sign I hang around my neck
I crave a field full of sunflowers // I crave a room full of familiarity
To be discarded is written through my sepia-tinged soul
All I want is my own place among the crowd

Was I more open before those first stares? .. .. ..
Before the schoolyard, the hospital, the footpath. With each drawnout
dissecting gaze, I withdrew. Soon, the trek
to belonging felt beyond me (I'd given in to "reality"
as if their looking defined anything). What I couldn't control
was how you would come for me, unravelling the shroud.

"...was how you would come for me." Unravelling the shroud?
You expected an AI generated shamanic avatar to levitate you instead?
Surprise is that's how you saw *this*—a non-living thing, of feint blue lines from desiccated bones?
A wonderment of disappearance in the cursory blink in the screen's white-blue glow?
Pulse doesn't need blooded, to be hard pressed against linimented linen to know it exists, *there*—
in the slough of others' disavowed words, words our deviant tongues rewild to glory.

I remain proud
despite the what-happened, so-brave, inspiring,
the better-off-dead—
despite the litany of strange looks and sideways glares
sticks and stones
and words that hurt but only hone me
into something sharper, clearer in purpose.
Yes, I know
the world seeks to erase us. Still, I refuse
to sink into the mire of it. We'll fight back
adapt and resist
write ourselves a better future, write ourselves
into history

(To) write ourselves a better future, (to) write ourselves into history,
to rest and watch time lift from edge to centre,
to practise the art of laughing into darkness, of laughing out of it. To practise.
Again, I close my eyes and build the path as I am walking it,
kneeling beside you, planting flagstones, my hand brushing up against yours every so often.
(Before us, a tract of paper, light, memory).

Labours of our crypthand slide into a DM depository,
the digital labyrinth of our deviant centaur,
where screamed scratchings, dreading caesura and confessional colons coalesce
Us, strapped and buckling to the letters as capital, as amulet
as we face their hardness equipping ourselves to soften
aware that letters don't fix, yet their worth lies in relief, no matter how temporary.

Strapped to the lack of a fix,   I only wanted
the relief of speaking. Writing   alone, it felt as if the letters
were the labours of my deviant   bones (or did they slide
out of the aether?). Yet my worth   was never a possession,
never private property – it's a way   for us to coalesce
(without disappearing into Us). Writing together, we matter,
we materialise. My ear (your ear) becomes our mouth.

Slowly ,,, slowly   coming to grips with all that is   /////slanted:
ancient timelines,   the leaf curling in my palm,   the 'get better'
barking from a speaker,   the pitching of the tiles   outside
my window. I was told there were a thousand ways to see   -to my transgression
none of which   I've tolerated   with any "real"   success
learning instead   to speak the colour   in this   scatter-
ing, in a message from a kindred stranger,   in this water as it bows   towards us both

Slanted, I am, among the tall straight human-built burrow -_- everything comes slowly.
Better than not at all, maybe, but my mind is muddled and my body <?> is read as ancient.
Outside, I look young, but my throat throttles my words, #8R0K3N meanings, I am barking
transgression with pitiful pleadings for others to hear me +2= acknowledge me///;/take my
success, not as inspiration, but instead as defiance, know that I M(&M) a battle cry. None
scatter at my strangeness (when I'm dreaming). My value ;_; is more than a tool for your learning.
Both my highs and lows deserve your warmth (campfire marshmallow$), eye M knot nothing-ing-ing

This disabled throat   This disabled mouth
This body   these bones   these bodies wholly
revealed   in the deviant dream of dawn   radiant
in the swell of disabled joy   limping and slanting
across the page   singing the mad battle cry
of crip rage and crip love   singing revolution
into history resting rising up   overturning
the old regime   of normalcy   for something
strange // something glorious //
something   new

Beau Windon, Andy Jackson, Michèle Saint-Yves, Robin M Eames & Ruby Hillsmith

Contributors

Alex Creece is a writer, editor, collage artist, and average kook living on Wadawurrung land. Alex's first book is *Potty Mouth, Potty Mouth* (Cordite Books, 2024).

Andy Jackson is a poet, creative writing teacher at the University of Melbourne, and a Patron of Writers Victoria. He was the inaugural Writing the Future of Health Fellow, has co-edited disability-themed issues of *Southerly* and *Australian Poetry Journal*, and is on the editorial team for disability poetry journal *Sunder*. He has featured at literary events and arts festivals across Australia, and on ABC's Radio National and the *7.30 Report*. Andy's latest poetry collection is *Human Looking*, which won the ALS Gold Medal and the Prime Minister's Literary Award for Poetry. He writes and rests on Dja Dja Wurrung country.

Angela Costi lives on Wurundjeri land. She is the author of five poetry collections, nine produced plays and performance texts, and is the co-author of community textbook, *Relocated*. Recent poetry and other writing are in *APJ, APA, Meanjin, Antipodes, Cordite, Hecate, Rochford Street Review, Meniscus, The Journal of Working-Class Studies* and the *Remnant* anthology as a finalist in the joanne burns Microlit Award. She lives with a rare genetic condition: multiple schwannomatosis. She is known as Αγγελικη Κωστη among the Cypriot Greek diaspora, which is her heritage.

Anna Jacobson is an award-winning writer and artist from Meanjin (Brisbane). Her memoir *How to Knit a Human* was published with NewSouth Publishing in 2024. *Amnesia Findings* won the Thomas Shapcott Poetry Prize. Anna's second illustrated poetry collection, *Anxious in a Sweet Store*, was published with Upswell in 2023. She holds a Doctor of Philosophy in Creative Writing from the Queensland University of Technology. She was a recipient of a Queensland Premier's Young Publishers and Writers Award and was a finalist in the Blake Art Prize, Olive Cotton Award, and Marie Ellis OAM Prize for Drawing. Anna's website is www.annajacobson.com.au

Beau Windon (he/ him) is a neurodivergent author of Wiradjuri heritage based in Naarm. He writes quirky stories about quirky people (including his quirky self) and poetry about all of the dark goo washing over his mind. He has been awarded a 2021 Writeability Fellowship, a 2022 residency from the City of Melbourne, and an arts grant from the Australia Council for the Arts. Beau's further creative non-fiction has been shortlisted in three categories for the Lord Mayor's Creative Writing Awards, winning the Self-Told Stories by Writers Living with Disability category and runner-up for the Indigenous Life Stories category. Recently, he was one of the winners of *Griffith Review*'s Emerging Voices 2023 competition. Beau has had personal essays published in *Griffith Review, Island, Archer, Mascara*'s Resilience Anthology, *VICE, Dear Lover*, and *Writers Victoria*. You can find out more about him at: beauwindon.com

Bron Bateman is an award-winning queer and crip poet, educator and editor from Boorloo (Perth). She has had three collections of poetry published and is in the editing phase of her fourth collection, with the working title of *Love Like This Isn't Harmless*. She has been published in journals and anthologies locally, nationally and internationally.

CB Mako is one of the founding members of the Disabled QBIPOC Collective along with Gemma Mahadeo, Nayook, and Pauline Vetuna. Based in Naarm, cubbie is also a contributor to the anthologies, *Growing up Disabled in Australia* and *Collisions: Fictions of the Future*, and *Mascara Literary Review*'s 'Resilience'. Winner of the Grace Marion Wilson Emerging Writers Competition, shortlisted in Overland's Fair Australia Prize, and longlisted in the Liminal Fiction Prize, cubbie's writings are in *The Suburban Review*, *Peril* Magazine and *Kill Your Darlings*, among others.

Esther Ottaway is the winner of the 2022 Tim Thorne Prize for Poetry and People's Choice Award in the Tasmanian Literary Awards. She also holds multiple national and international prizes and shortlistings, including the Montreal, Bridport, Mslexia, MPU International, and Tom Collins Prizes. Esther is noted for her powerful poems about women's experiences, including birth, motherhood, divorce, and autism. She has co-edited *Australian Poetry Journal*, published widely in leading national and international journals, judged competitions, and is widely anthologised, including in *Thirty Australian Poets* (UQP). Her third collection is *She Doesn't Seem Autistic* (Puncher & Wattmann 2023). She lives in lutruwita/Tasmania.

Gaele Sobott lives on Dharug land, Sydney. Her books include *Colour Me Blue* and *My Longest Round*. She has published short stories and poems in literary magazines and anthologies, and her poetry animations continue to win international acclaim. Gaele is the recipient of a 2023 Australia Council Fellowship, 2021 Varuna Writers Space Fellowship and 2020 City of Sydney fellowship. She has a PhD in literature from the University of Hull, UK.

Gemma Mahadeo moved to Australia in 1987. Their written work and multimedia work has been published nationally, both online and in print. They are a founding member of The Disabled QBIPOC Collective, along with CB Mako, Hannah Morphy-Walsh, and Pauline Vetuna. When not writing, they occasionally make music, drink lots of tea and beer, and fuss over cats.

Heather Taylor-Johnson lives and writes on Kaurna land near Port Adelaide. Her most recent poetry books are a verse novel titled *Rhymes with Hyenas* and a collection titled *Alternative Hollywood Ending*. Her second novel, *Jean Harley was Here*, was shortlisted for the Readings Prize for New Fiction, and she won the Island Nonfiction Prize. She writes about the body and about art, which are often the same thing, and is the editor of *Shaping the Fractured Self: Poetry of Chronic Illness and Pain*. She is an Adjunct Research Fellow at the J M Coetzee Centre for Creative Practice.

Jasper Peach is a trans, non-binary and disabled writer, speaker and parent. They are passionate about equitable access and inclusion, focused on the dismantling of misplaced shame via storytelling. Their written work has been published in *The Age, HireUp, The Big Issue, Archer, The Guardian, Verandah, Australian Poetry Journal, Meanjin,* and on ABC and SBS online. With a background in Auslan interpreting, broadcasting and civil celebrancy, writing has continued their personal trend of being all about communication and community. Their first book, *You'll be a Wonderful Parent* (Hardie Grant 2023), is a celebration of rainbow families of all kinds.

Jess Kapuscinski-Evans is a writer/performer and sings with "crip folk" trio the Bearbrass Asylum Orchestra. She recently formed the Waiting Room Arts Company and enjoys playing with existing texts and pop culture.

Katerina Bryant is a writer based on Kaurna land. Her first book, *Hysteria: A Memoir of Illness, Strength and Women's Stories Throughout History* (NewSouth), was published in 2020.

Kerri Shying belongs to the Wiradjuri people and is of Chinese-Australian ancestry. A life of slow work with hidden people has given her respect for the small stories, the hard places. She has published in the Roland Robinson Awards and appears in the *Women of Words* series with Papatuanuku Press, Hunter Writers Centre's *Grieve* and *Inclusion* series, and a variety of other journals, including *Billy Blue, Satellite* and *Users News*. She writes, always, and makes art, and is the author of *Elevensies* and *Know Your Country*.

Kit Kavanagh-Ryan is a queer crip poet and academic based in Melbourne, whose recent publications include works in *Cordite, Australian Poetry Journal,* and spoken word collaborations with Australian musician, David Bridie. In 2024, they completed their PhD at Deakin University. When not falling over, they think and write about the weird and lovely ways bodies and minds work together. While falling over, they're still doing that, just slower.

Leah Robertson is a writer and visual artist residing on unceded Boonwurrung land. Her work has been published and exhibited in various Australian journals and galleries. It is inherently informed by her experience living with complex psychosocial disability.

Living with disability on Kaurna Country, **Michèle Saint-Yves** primarily writes for performance – stage, screen and poetry – and on occasion has directed and produced plays and short films, with several short stories and poems published in journals and anthologies. Michèle published her first book of poetry, *Lament,* with Friendly Street Poets Inc in 2021.

Rachael Wenona Guy is a multidisciplinary artist who works across a range of media, including poetry, performance, visual theatre, animation and puppetry. Her writing has been published in journals and anthologies in Australia and overseas, including *Overland, Sleepers Almanac, Mascara, Negative Capability,* and *Australian Poetry Journal.* Her collaborations with poet Andy Jackson have appeared at Queensland Poetry Festival, Castlemaine State Festival, Berlin Flash Film Festival and Clifden Arts Week, Ireland. She currently lives in Central Victoria where she writes and draws in a backyard room surrounded by trees and sweet clutter. Rachael writes to examine the fraught and delicate spaces of existence and make sense of the battered oddments of subjectivity, both beautiful and unsettling.

Robin M Eames is a queercrip poet and historian living on Gadigal land. Their work has been published in *Overland, Meanjin, Cordite, Health & History,* and *APJ,* among others. They research 19th century trans histories.

Ruby Hillsmith is a writer, editor and poet living on Wurundjeri land. She was the 2020 Writers Victoria Writeability Poetry Fellow, a 2020 Wheeler Centre Hot Desk Fellow, and co-editor-in-chief of the 31st edition of RMIT's *Visible Ink*. She mentors Writers Victoria's 2024 Writeability Goes Online writers group and is an associate editor at *The Suburban Review*. She can be found at rubyhillsmith.com.

Sam Drummond grew up in country Victoria before moving to Melbourne to study arts and law at Monash University. He began his career as a broadcaster and producer on community, commercial and public radio, before moving into politics and finally into law. Sam now specialises in discrimination and human rights law. As a disabled person, he has a particular interest in removing legal barriers for people with disabilities. When he is not parenting, writing or working, he can be found swimming laps of Melbourne's outdoor pools, tending to his native garden or discovering parts of the world he didn't get to experience as a kid.

Sarah Stivens is a poet and editor living on Boon Wurrung/Bunurong land. She is the founding editor of *Sunder Journal,* and her work appears in *Cordite, Australian Poetry Journal, Baby Teeth Journal, Catalyst,* and other outlets. She was the 2022 Ray Koppe/ASA Varuna fellow, and a 2022 Writeability fellow. She writes about mental illness, disability, and rural identities. When not writing, you'll find her swearing at her sewing machine.

Index to works by author

www.ingramcontent.com/pod-product-compliance
Lightning Source LLC
Chambersburg PA
CBHW041956050726
47507CB00033B/411
9781923099326